Sh*tty Mom

Sh*tty Mom

THE PARENTING GUIDE FOR THE REST OF US

LAURIE KILMARTIN
KAREN MOLINE
ALICIA YBARBO
MARY ANN ZOELLNER

ABRAMS IMAGE, NEW YORK

To our moms: JoAnn Kilmartin, Gloria Moline,
Irene Ybarbo, and Ann Knight

Published in 2012 by Abrams Image
An imprint of ABRAMS

Cataloging-in-Publication Data has been applied for and may be
obtained from the Library of Congress.

ISBN: 978-1-4197-0459-8

Editor: Jennifer Levesque
Designer: Kara Strubel
Production Manager: Erin Vandeveer

Printed and bound in the United States
10 9 8 7 6 5 4 3 2 1

Abrams Image books are available at special discounts when purchased
in quantity for premiums and promotions as well as fundraising or
educational use. Special editions can also be created to specification. For
details, contact specialsales@abramsbooks.com or the address below.

THE ART OF BOOKS SINCE 1949

115 West 18th Street
New York, NY 10011
www.abramsbooks.com

ACKNOWLEDGMENTS

This book would not have come to be were it not for the brilliant insights of the indefatigably wondrous Yfat Reiss Gendell. Her stellar team at Foundry— Stephanie Abou, the foreign rights director; Rachel Hecht, the foreign rights associate; and editorial assistants Cecilia Campbell Westlind and Erica Walker— was also invaluable. Much gratitude is owed to the incomparable Madeleine Morel, who brought us to Yfat and made this partnership possible.

We were lucky to find a kindred spirit in our editor at Abrams, Jennifer Levesque. Her team—managing editor David Blatty, art director Sarah Gifford, designer Kara Strubel, and publicist Claire Bamundo—are consummate professionals.

Many thanks as well to the fantastically imaginative Christoph Niemann, whose cover illustration brought *Sh*tty Mom* to life.

We would also like to thank the following:

Laurie Kilmartin:
Thanks to my dad, Ron, my kid (name withheld so he can distance himself from me), and the sitters, Klare and Kathleen. Neither of the babysitting chapters is about you.

Karen Moline:
My magical son, Emmanuel, for giving me countless new ways to mess up. Thanks to Sara, Kassaundra, and Diane, the babysitters whose college loans are now smaller because of the many hours they put in, and moms deluxe Deborah Feingold, Maggie Alderson, and Eve Blouin, who bring laughter into our world even when life isn't always funny.

Alicia Ybarbo:
My partner in parenting, Mark Zimmerman: you are such a loving husband and father. I thank you and love you. And to Goose and Scootie: nothing makes me happier than being your mommy.

Mary Ann Zoellner:
My husband, Alexander; and my two little girls, Beanie and Pinkie. Your humor, support, and love make each day better than the last.

CONTENTS

OTHER PEOPLE ARE HORRIBLE

AND SOMETIMES THE ASSHOLE IS YOU

OTHER MOMS

NOMS (NON-MOMS)

YOU AREN'T PARANOID, EVERYONE DOES HATE YOUR BABY

AWKWARD CONVERSATIONS

WE DIDN'T FORGET ABOUT YOU, SH*TTY DADS!

YES, IT'S OK TO HATE THE ZOO

SH*TTY MOM: HERE TO HELP

INTRODUCTION

Children.

They want everything you have, and they want it now. They don't care about ruining your abs or killing your sex life, and they sure as hell don't give a shit that you only slept four hours last night. Kids—and their proto-versions, *babies*—don't care about the mortgage, saving for retirement, or the way they add six inches to the length of your breasts. They want you to quit your job and pay attention to them. Babies hate your friends, and they wish you would take that damn dog to the pound—preferably one that euthanizes. Any person, physical need, or dream that pulls focus for even five seconds is their natural enemy and must be crushed with loud, endless cries.

If that's not bad enough, babies are also completely helpless. They have soft spots and weak necks. They can't run from predators—in fact, they can't even throw a frozen dinner in the microwave. You would think that any creature so dependent on others for survival would be grateful to their parents and/or guardians.

Not babies.

Selfish and suicidal, babies try to kill themselves twenty-four hours a day. They reach for knives, lick the Lysol bottle, and roll over on their stomachs at night. Every morning, babies call each other on the phone to discuss new ways to get you into trouble with Child Protective Services. In their secret Yahoo e-mail group, the lead baby will write, "Stick your tongue on an electric outlet," and the follower babies will chime in with the best ways to do it. They are the animal kingdom's most mean-spirited young. When you bring one home from the hospital or an orphanage in China, never forget that your baby's only goal in life is to ruin you.

Sh*tty Mom is about how to survive babies, and what they grow into: children. *Sh*tty Mom* is about shortcuts and parenting with 40 percent effort. It's about doing a half-assed job, but doing it well enough so that no one but you notices. It's about not letting that baby win every battle.

Are you a Sh*tty Mom?
Take our quiz.

* Did you hate kids before you had one?

* Do you hate them even more now (except yours)?

* When people say, "Being a mom is so exhausting," do you think, "Not the way I do it"?

* Are you willing to sacrifice some of your child's happiness so you can sleep for another hour?

* Do you ignore any pediatrician's orders that you don't agree with?

* Does your kid have to have a fever above 100 degrees before you'll keep him home?

* If your kid *does* have a 100-degree fever, do you debate raising the "keep him home" fever ceiling to 101 degrees?

* If you accept the premise that there are two kinds of moms at the park, "Plays with Her Children Mom" and "Texts from the Bench Mom," then are you the latter?

* If you had to choose between a babysitter who:
a) plays with your children but arrives late
b) ignores your children but arrives on time, would you choose *b*? (No fair saying you'd make "*a*" come early.)

* Did becoming a mom make you realize that your own mother was even worse than you thought?

If you answered yes to three or more questions, you are a Sh*tty Mom. If you answered yes to all of them, you are a hero.

YOUR CHILDREN WANT TO RUIN YOU

Road Trip with Your Kids: Multiply How Bad You Think It Will Be by a Thousand, Then Add Ten Million

First, let's figure out how this happened. What series of bad decisions led to this terrible morning, where you are packing the minivan with juice boxes, sliced apples, cheese sandwiches, edible Goldfish, small coolers, chapter books, crayons, and portable DVD players? How could it be that, hours from now, a smart cookie such as yourself will be changing your baby's diaper in a truck-stop bathroom usually reserved for $20 hand jobs?

Did you fail to consult Google Maps before you agreed to go to the in-laws for the holidays? Or Disney World as a family? If you live in Ohio, did you forget that, in order to get to Florida, you have to drive through Kentucky, Tennessee, and Georgia?

That is some brain fart, sister. Here's a few things to try:

* **Cancel.** And not just this Thanksgiving, but every Thanksgiving, until your youngest is at least six.

* **Skype.** Hire the Geek Squad to set up Skype on your mother-in-law's computer. It will cost less than what you'll spend on gas.

* **Check airfares.** It's possible to get reasonable last-minute airfares (if you're not traveling on a holiday). While flying with kids is its own kind of hell, it is at least a shorter one.

If you are already driving:

* **Save time, pee on the side of the road.** If you have more than one kid, you can't pull into a gas station every time a juice box is digested. Pit stops can add as much as an hour to a trip, when you factor in the tantrums that come from saying no to mini-mart candy.

   Find a nice ditch, off the side of a wide shoulder, and teach your little one to squat or pull it out. Being able to pee outdoors is an essential skill that every American ought to have. It's how many of us will urinate in the future, as our nation slides further into debt. Soon bathrooms will become like universities, with the public ones defunded and the private ones hugely expensive.

* **Give up and turn around.** This is a golden opportunity to let the kids know that Mom doesn't take shit. Because let's face it, somewhere along the way, you've lost their respect.

   You've threatened to leave a movie theater when they've acted like brats, but then stayed because it was less a hassle. Over the years, you've become exhausted and predictable. They know how to play you. Your bite is toothless.

   Well, today the joke's on them, because you didn't want to go to Disney/Thanks/Christ/Hannu/Flags/Land anyway. This time when you yell, "I swear to God, if you hit your sister one more time, I'm turning this car around," you will actually turn that car around. They will be shocked at your coldheartedness. They will scream and cry, but you will not cave, because this time it's easy to follow through.

   And then, they will fear you.

* **Make them suck it up.** Our kids are unskilled in the dark arts of entertaining themselves during a road trip. They sit comfortably in special seats, with their sippy cups

lodged in convenient cup holders. DVD players unfold from the minivan's ceiling, and they are entertained like child emperors in the last days of Rome. If you can handle the whining, turn the radio to your favorite station and teach them how to be alone with their thoughts by providing no distractions at all.

 Remember: This time you will "turn this SUV around RIGHT NOW!"

Other Things Your Kid Will Try to Clean with the Gas Station Squeegee

Oh, the little ones, they love to help out at the gas station. Hold the gas pump, then wash the car with a squeegee that's been sitting in gray water for two days. After your daughter polishes your car, she will only want more. Depending on how attentive you are, she'll hit one or all of these targets:

* The ground
* Other cars
* Your shoes
* Your car's recently conditioned leather interior
  (oh, she's in the car now)
* The GPS
* The backup, handwritten directions to Disney World
* Her baby sister's hair
* All the orange slices. All of them.

CHAPTER 2

You're Home with the Kid and You Have a Conference Call in Ten Minutes

Whether you're working from home because your kid is sick, you freelance, or you're still looking for a job, there's one thing you must do during a conference call: Get your kid to shut up.

Children hate anyone who takes your attention away from them. Like animals that can sense an impending earthquake, children can tell when you're about to say something very important to a client. They have a superpower, and they use it for evil. You must prepare.

BEFORE THE CALL.

Lock the front and back doors. Make sure your child can't get out of the house. It's possible that, if she has a tantrum, you will be forced to hide in your bedroom closet. You need to know that your daughter won't run into the street while you pitch ideas from under the winter blankets.

Prepare diversions. Set everything up before your child sees you holding the phone.

Food bribery. Now is not the time to avoid corn syrup. Better that your child gets cavities or diabetes than you lose your job. Ice cream, candy bars, chocolate, chips, gum balls, chips, leftover pizza: Any food that seems like a bad idea is a great idea. Ice cream should be pre-scooped into bowls, candy bars unwrapped, pizza reheated, all of it ready to be passed out, mid-whine.

Fill two to three sippy cups. Instead of pouring during the call, grab the next cup on the assembly line. This child will not win.

Eventually, you will train her to love your conference calls.

Put on a DVD. And have four alternates standing by. Even if your child loves her Thomas the Tank Engine DVD, she will demand you put in Winnie the Pooh, just to test your loyalty. (Because having her wasn't enough.)

DURING THE CALL.

Hide. Stay out of her line of sight—let her sink into the food and TV. You have between ten and thirty minutes before she starts looking for you.

Mute the phone. After she finds you, put the phone on mute. She is about to launch her "Mom, I have to go potty!" grenade. It's better that your coworkers don't hear you than they do hear your child.

Give yourself permission to go nuclear. No one is going to call CPS if you end up barricading your kid in her bedroom. In fact, the other people on the call will wish that you'd done it sooner.

 Remember: "If my kids are still alive at the end of the day, I've done my job." —*Roseanne*

CHAPTER 3

Screens Con: Don't Let Your Kid Become a PDA-hole

Look, you and me—we're ruined. Any parent who's Generation X or younger grew up with computers, laptops, video games, cell phones, and now smartphones. We surf the internet and text while we watch TV. We're always hovered over a screen, tapping and typing, never giving anything our full attention. We're self-centered and awful.

But it's OK, because we're grown-ups. We spent a few of our formative years playing with tangible objects and drawing with crayons. We're allowed to be PDA-holes because we've earned it.

Our kids, however, have not.

Boredom is character building. How else will your oldest child figure out how hard she needs to pinch your youngest child until she cries? Do you *want* a baby sister who wasn't tortured by her older sister? That's unnatural.

It is the bored child who discovers that boogers are salty, Sharpie pens work on walls, and that a steady hand can tease the legs off of a living fly. It is the bored child who will eventually slide a hand down his or her pants and meets that amazing, soon-to-be best friend that lives just inches below the belly button. Does the boy whose mom has the Cake Doodle app on her iPhone even know he has a penis?

All iPhones, iPads, and iPods (and their non-Apple counterparts) should be kept out of reach, for as long as possible. No one's suggesting you get rid of your devices. That would be ridiculous and unreasonable. It would mean you would have to use a landline. Just keep them away from your kids. Here's a few ideas:

* **Pretend the device is broken.** It's never too soon to teach kids that, in life, things break. Electronics, televisions, hearts. Life is pain. Later, at your convenience, you can "fix" it. See, kids? Hearts mend. Moms heal. Life goes on.

* **Pretend the device is lost.** Ask them to complete a chore, and in exchange for a good job, you'll find it for them. Now the toys are put away, and you're a hero.

* **Pretend the battery is dead.** For when you're tired of pretending it's broken. This only buys you the amount of time it normally takes to charge the battery.

 Remember: All these solutions demand that you look into your children's eyes and lie. Be strong.

Ways to Rationalize Your Child's Increase in Screen Time

You have a bad feeling about your toddler and screens. In the back of your mind something isn't right. Well, there's only one thing you can do about those fears: Rationalize them away.

He is learning how to:
* Count.
* Use a touchscreen.
* Count things with a touchscreen, then kill them.

He is not:
* Putting sunglasses on the dog.
* Making scratch marks on his sister's leg with his fingernails.
* Trying to duplicate the scratch marks, but this time with his toenails.

And, he may grow up to be:
* An app developer.
* A computer programmer.
* An overweight gamer who never moves out of the house. Wait, who said that? Oh shut up, "back of my mind."

CHAPTER 4

Screens Pro: iCan Finally Take My Kid to a Restaurant. Thank You, Angry Birds!

You know how you resist something solely because it's popular? Because you're not a drone that falls in-line with whatever's trending on Google. Then you try that popular thing and it's not too bad. And you're embarrassed it took you this long to admit that, for example, Katy Perry isn't terrible? Well, the preceding chapter was written before its shitty author broke down and tried Angry Birds.

Oh my.

Please enjoy an opposing view on PDAs, held by the same person.

If your kids' screen cherry is already broken, you've lost the war. They've tasted the sweet thrill that comes from killing a pig with a well-flung bird. Now they're aware of a world beyond the woodsy goodness of Melissa & Doug.

They want more.

Luckily, you're not alone. Go to an Applebee's or a T.G.I. Friday's and you'll see whole families eating in silence, enjoying their screen-lit dinner. We've all surrendered to our glowing overlords.

Oh, not you? You've held out, huh? Your daughter isn't going to have one of those things for a loooooong time. Well. Aren't you the cocky one.

For your plan to work, you need other mothers to do the same. And they won't. Your daughter will attend school with their children, and these kids will know she's "different." Her reasonable attention span and ability to read something longer than a text will mark her as Other. She will be ostracized and mocked until, one day, her fingertips will find a classmate's screen. She'll tap once. Twice. A game will open, and within an hour, she'll be at level 16.

Maybe not this year, maybe not next year. But surely by second grade. And then you'll be one of us.

The good news is that the addictive nature of a PDA will increase your parental powers. Your kids will become junkies and you, their dealer.

Imagine for a moment what it must be like to dole out coke to a cokehead. That's a cokehead that you can control. That's a cokehead who will brush his teeth the first time he's asked. Who will be quiet at a Starbucks and engrossed during the aforementioned seven-hour drive.

Don't pretend the iPhone is lost, broken, or forgotten—that makes you look weak. And a good dealer never looks weak. Instead, let your cokeheads know that their connection, Mom, has downloaded the smartphone equivalent of 10 kilos of sweet stuff from Bolivia. And they will get it after they eat their peas.

Managing the flow of demand: This is how nations are built and rebellions are crushed.

You pimp, you.

 Remember: We're all going to hell together.

PDA Lies You Tell Your Kids

They see you using it, despite that it's "No Screen Sunday." And they want to know why they can't.

"Mom's just checking her e-mail."
Despite your new rule, there you are, tapping away. And you're not checking e-mail. No one e-mailed you. Well, two people did, but one of them is a "horny MILF" who thinks you are a guy and lonely. The other is your husband and he doesn't count.

"Let's listen to the radio."
A driving quandary. You want to listen to Marc Maron's podcast, *WTF*, on your iPhone, but it's too dirty for your four-year-old daughter, so you can't plug the phone into the speakers. So you put the radio on and slip the phone between your legs. You stick an earbud in your left ear (facing the driver's side window) and leave the right ear unbudded. As far as your daughter knows, you and she are both suffering through corporate radio together. Enjoy that lie as long as you can. The moment she notices that little white wire dangling from your left ear, not even remotely blending in with your brown hair, she will never trust you again.

"Mom wants to make sure this game is appropriate for you."
Oh really? Then why are you still wearing earbuds? You're not done listening to WTF. Everyone knows it.

BUT SOMETIMES THEY ARE AWESOME

CHAPTER 5

How to React if You Think Your Child Might Be Gay (*Hint: Celebrate*)

Sometimes you can tell. Your son likes "girl toys," or your daughter doesn't. Your husband doesn't want to talk about it, but your Spidey sense is telling you that your kid might be gay. What do you do?

Pop the champagne!

Your gay kid may be the best thing that ever happened to you.

GO WITH IT.

If you can be fully supportive of your gay child, you will be loved. Loved, adored, and worshipped. (And possibly impersonated in a drag show.) And your gay kid's gay friends will wish you were their mom. They will remember you on Mother's Day, and after your death, your funeral will be jam-packed with good-looking men and strong-shouldered women.

DON'T TRY TO "STRAIGHTEN" YOUR GAY CHILD.

Not only will she remain gay, but one day she may write a scathing memoir about her childhood. When it's turned into a movie, the "mom" will be played by someone who is shorter, fatter, and more wrinkled than you are.

CLOSETED GAYS ARE NOT HAPPY PEOPLE.

Forcing your gay kid to live a lie will backfire. Kids who repress their homosexuality often grow up to become disgraced pastors

(Ted Haggard), hypocritical lawyers (Roy Cohn), insane dictators (Adolf Hitler, according to some sources), or Scientologists (no example provided due to potential litigation).

Your child deserves better.

PREPARE FOR BATTLE.

It's likely that the five-year-old boy who looks so adorable wearing your sleep bra will, in his teen years, be bullied by an asshole. It's wrong and it's unfair, but it's common. Sh*tty Mom believes that, like Israel, gay kids should be allowed to preemptively strike if they feel threatened. Gay bashing would end quickly if gangs of tough gay kids were allowed to roam the streets, beating the crap out of problematic straight kids.

Try to interest your kid in some kind of martial arts. If he can enter middle school with a black belt, the school bully might skip him and move on to the kid who's really asking for it: the nerd.

(FYI: Nerds should remain closeted until they are accepted into Stanford.)

ADAM AND STEVE CAN'T MAKE A BABY EVE.

What the Christian right hates about gay couples is what parents should love: They can't procreate. Unlike your sister, whose straight daughter will be alarmingly boy crazy when she's fourteen, you won't be up nights, worrying that your gay kid is legs up in the backseat of a truck somewhere, getting pregnant.

Gay people have to go out of their way to have children. They hire surrogates, they adopt. Some of them will even put David Crosby's sperm in their vaginas (!). All of those procedures are planned and costly. If your gay kid ever does have a baby, at least you won't be stuck raising it while she's out partying instead of studying for her GED.

And what if you are wrong and your kid ends up being straight? Better luck next time.

Remember: Stereotypes don't come out of nowhere. It's possible that your gay daughter will attend a Division 1 school on a softball scholarship or your gay son will style your hair. Forever. For free.

Kick-ass Moms of Gay Kids

Cher Well, technically Cher's son, Chaz, is a straight male. However, he started out as a lesbian named Chastity, so Cher gets an honorable mention.

Stephanie Seymour The former supermodel has an openly gay son named Peter Brant II. As a twosome, they caused a slight sensation when photographed on a beach in what some people described as a semi-incestuous embrace. In a written defense of his mother, Peter mentioned that he is gay. At the time, he was a senior in high school. It's tough to come out at that age, but we're guessing his mom made it easier.

Alice Hoagland Mark Bingham died on 9/11. He was a rugby player and one of the passengers on United 93. He helped overpower the hijackers, and possibly prevented the plane from crashing into the Capitol Building. Afterwards, his mom, Alice Hoagland, exhibited striking composure and grace while speaking to the media about her son. She didn't make Mark's homosexuality the focal point of her memories, but she also didn't shy away from it.

Betty DeGeneres Ellen's mom, Betty, wrote a book with her daughter, and they talked about the coming-out process. Betty also appears frequently on *Ellen*, and she was the first nongay spokesperson for the Human Rights Campaign's Coming Out Project.

CHAPTER 6

When Your Kid Is a Different Race/Ethnicity Than You

First of all, scoot over. You have a story to tell and Sh*tty Mom is all ears. As far as we can tell, one of the following scenarios must have gone down:

YOU HAD SEX WITH AN OTHER-RACE MAN.

Well, aren't you the naughty one. Giving your parents a heart attack when you dragged home that black/white/Asian/Hispanic/Arab/Indian/Jewish/Native American/Pacific Islander guy from college.

You are ahead of the curve. Sometime in the middle of the twenty-first century, America will cease to be a white majority country. Your nonwhite or half-white or Hispanic-but-no-one-thinks-that's-white kids will be the majority. An added bonus is that mixed race kids are often gorgeous. They take the best features from both parents and chuck the rest. The addition of new DNA is like restarting a frozen family tree.

America is a small country. This fact is illuminated during almost every election cycle when genealogists discover that the candidates are related. George W. Bush and John Kerry are ninth cousins, twice removed. Dick Cheney and Barack Obama are eighth cousins. Look, if those two are related, we're all related. Dipping your toe in a new gene pool may prevent you from accidentally banging a cousin. (Because if you're going to bang your cousin, it should be on purpose.)

Good for you.

SOMEONE'S GREAT-GREAT-GRANDMOTHER HAD SEX WITH AN OTHER-RACE MAN AND IT'S JUST SHOWING UP NOW.

Way back when, one of your grannies got around. The evidence lay dormant for a few generations until, one day, out came your baby with different textured hair, or lighter or darker skin. The difference between you and your kid may not be as obvious, but you'll still get the occasional odd look when your brown kid shouts "Mom!" at the park, and pale, freckle-faced you shows up, saying, "What?"

YOU HAVE ADOPTED.

Hello, hero. Here's what strangers know about you: You're patient, generous, and good-hearted. They know you waited for a baby and that one day you got a call that changed your life. More than anyone, they know you wanted that baby. What strangers don't know is where you got your other-race child and, my, are they curious! They'll crack open Google Maps and rattle off Pacific Rim countries that are a potential match for your Asian daughter.

"China? Korea? Vietnam? Cambodia? Thailand?"

Only you can put them out of their Rand-McMisery and say, "San Francisco."

Now you are an expert on a culture that you'd previously only encountered at parades or restaurants. There is only one thing left to learn:

HOW TO STYLE YOUR KID'S HAIR.

You might be able to wing it with Caucasian or Asian hair, but African hair is serious business and must not be taken lightly. (See the Chris Rock documentary *Good Hair*.) Right behind it in degree of difficulty is red hair, depending on the curl. (Sorry to the Gingers that "red" isn't capitalized like "Caucasian," "Asian," and "African." And it probably doesn't help that "Ginger" is.)

Depending on where you live, head uptown or downtown to an appropriate beauty salon. Bring your kid and let a stylist show you what to do.

 Remember: There's no better way to show your child that you love her unconditionally than to learn how to comb her hair.

My Kids, My Husband, and I Are the Same Race/Ethnicity. Am I from the 1950s?

No, you are still of this millennium. But understand that Sh*tty Mom's Mexican-Irish son is coming for your Jewish daughter, and you can't stop him.

CHAPTER 7

It's Come to Your Attention
That Your Kid Is Merely Average

Your kid is three, maybe four years old. During playdates, you've noticed that he isn't the intellectual pack leader. He's not dumb, but he's not as quick with the puzzles. He knows his A-B-Ds. He is able to count to ten if you don't include six. You're close to admitting that your child may not be fast-tracked into the gifted program.

You luck out.

Based purely on anecdotal evidence, average kids grow up to be normal and well-adjusted adults. Just going by recent high school reunions, it's apparent that the class fuckups overwhelmingly hail from one of two groups: kids from bad families and kids from the gifted program. In fact, this chapter should be called "What If Your Child Is Gifted?" Because those are the moms who ought to be worried.

When you tell gifted kids they can be president, they'll calculate the odds with their big brains and say no. Soon they'll stop believing anything you say. You're just another upbeat liar who can't comprehend even basic statistics. But dumb kids will believe you every time.

Ronald Reagan was a C student. Did his mother panic and send him to Kumon four times a week? No. She accepted that he was a charmer with good hair, and understood that was enough.

But if you're reading this book, you probably don't want a C student. You want an A student. You know: like Ronald Reagan's vice president (and the one-term president) George H. W. Bush. Yes, him. Straight A's look good on paper, but they don't always get you a second term. (Or smart kids.)

Average kids inherently understand that they don't have the goods. They develop other skills precisely because they can't get an A-plus on a paper that was begun the night before it was due. They grow into college students who can study for a test and into competent grown-ups who can install a kitchen backsplash and use a slow cooker.

When an average kid scores 2000 on the new SATs, they are thrilled. Gifted kids are depressed. They think they should've scored a perfect 2400, what with all their gifts and Latin classes. Inevitably, they drift into a life of hopeless ennui, overqualified for their jobs and often working at companies started by an average kid.

How can you recession-proof an average kid's future?

* **Team sports.** Get them involved in team sports—that's key. Ice hockey, not figure skating. Water polo, not diving. Basketball, not track. The sports team is a laboratory where your average kid can learn how to boss her future employees around. (Note: This advice will be completely contradicted in chapter 12, "Organized Sports Might Be Great for the Kids, but They Suck for You.")

* **Guitar lessons.** Hey, someone has to be the band's bass player, right? To put it in Van Halen terms, your average kid will never be an Eddie, but he could most certainly be a Michael Anthony.

Of course, many gifted kids are happy, have great jobs, and make lots of money. Play along, we're trying to cheer up the moms of average kids here.

 Remember: It's the dumb kids with trust funds that we really need to be worried about.

Is Your Child "Slow" or Is He a Boy?

Moms of boys usually have a stroke when they meet a girl who is the same age as their son. Four-year-old girls speak. And not with guttural tongue-flapping and fart noises, but with language. Girls use words, they create sentences and understand metaphors. Listening to your son after you've spent time with a girl will make you wonder when he became Jodie Foster in *Nell*.

Don't panic. Your boy could be quite gifted—just not compared to an average girl. Language disparities between boys and girls tend to even out by the time the boys are in their mid-forties (earlier, if they've had therapy).

STOP

NOT

TAKING

THE

EASY WAY

OUT

CHAPTER 8

Ten-Second Rule:
Pacifier on the Ground

Ugh. This is one of those mothery tasks that is done for appearance's sake only. Public streets are not covered in anthrax and cocaine. Your baby will be fine if the pacifier goes right back into her mouth. In fact, she may grow stronger after ingesting the street's unique nutrients. And while it is never advised to deliberately lick the sidewalk, no one has ever died from it.

But who has time to explain common sense to strangers? The next time you drop the binky, follow this two-step process.

Look around. Did anyone see the pacifier fall?

1. *If no:* Wipe the pacifier on your shirt. Stick it back in baby's mouth.
2. *If yes:* Damn. You have a witness, who may just be filming it on her iPhone so that she can put it up on YouTube, tagged with the search term "terrible mother." Well, the joke's on her, because no one's going to get you on film being a bad mother. All you have to do is add a second step to number one. After you wipe the pacifier on your shirt, stick it in your mouth. Take the hit, like a good soldier. Then stick it back in baby's mouth. YouTube disaster averted.

 Remember: If you are the kind of person who thought to bring a backup pacifier, this book is not for you. Sorry.

CHAPTER 9

How to Sleep In Until Nine A.M. Every Weekend

Behind your back, the other moms call you lazy. They buckle their broods into the minivans on a Sunday morning, late for a soccer game four towns over. They spot your car, parked defiantly in the driveway. Through your curtains, they see your child sitting on the floor, rapt, watching *Dora the Explorer* on your giant TV. Anyone resembling a mother is not visible.

It's almost as if you're still asleep.

Bitch.

Look. It matters not why you're tired. You could be a single mom, an old mom, an anemic mom, a works-two-jobs mom, or an "alcoholic who hasn't hit bottom yet" mom.

The important thing is that, once your baby started sleeping through the night, you realized that if you didn't get some rest, you were gonna die. Your kid is four now. In China, four-year-olds have jobs. Surely yours can entertain herself for a few hours while you sleep.

LEAVE BREAKFAST OUT THE NIGHT BEFORE.

Friday and Saturday nights should be like Christmas Eve. Instead of leaving a plate of cookies for Santa, you'll be leaving a plate of something breakfast-y for the kids. Something that won't go bad when left out during the hours between your bedtime and their wake time. (You can also leave it all in a small ice chest. Put a bow on top—it will be like opening a present.)

* **Whole apples** (don't cut them, otherwise they'll brown, and then there'll be a knock on your door about "old apples")
* **Cheese cubes** (in a ziplock bag)
* **Juice in sippy cups**—two per child
* **Peanut butter sandwiches,** or whatever you use as a peanut butter substitute
* **Cookies.** Soon, they will learn the principle known as Sh*tty Mom's Razor: Mom + asleep = cookies and cartoons. (You can save the nutritional breakfast for weekdays.)

ENTERTAINMENT.

Preface: This is a waste of energy, and not Al Gore approved.

We are assuming your kid knows how to push the remote's Play button. Leave the TV on overnight (sorry, future generations). Freeze the DVR on the opening frame of a ninety-plus-minute movie like *Curious George*. Leave the remote in plain sight. If, on his way to wake up Mom at 6:30 A.M., he sees the guy in the yellow outfit on TV, and that big red Play button on the remote, he will forget all about you.

If you don't have a DVR or don't have a good movie saved on it yet, leave cartoons on all night. The downside is each cartoon lasts just thirty minutes. Unless the next one starts immediately, your kid may see the commercial break as a time to go get Mom.

IF YOUR CHILDREN TRY TO WAKE YOU UP, YOU MUST FEIGN SLEEP.

They might sneak into your room and whisper. Under no circumstances should you look at them, acknowledge their presence with a half-smile, or even move. They might go away. But if they see even the whites of your eyes, they will consider you awake and theirs to torture. This means you pee in a cup so they don't hear you shuffle off to the bathroom. Always keep a clean Big Gulp cup under the bed.

"LET MOM GO BACK TO SLEEP" IS
NOT IN THEIR VOCABULARY.

If you give in to one request (i.e., making breakfast), you might as well get up because you are done for. Kids don't "let" you go back to sleep. Like a band of '70s-era terrorists, their demands will only increase in scope and impracticality. Instead of unmarked bills and a plane to Algeria, your kids will ask for more toast, then milk, and finally a castle and a horsey. When you point out the latter two are impossible, they will promise to release all of the hostages if you wake up and play with them.

Your sleep time is over.

ONE MOM'S "LAZY" IS THE SH*TTY MOM'S
"UNSTRUCTURED."

It's not easy—almost no one will support you. But your lack of participation is a rebellion. No lessons, no classes, no games. This is active resistance. You're like a freedom fighter, in pajamas. Your Monday–Fridays are busy and American, but your weekends are all France.

 Remember: Sh*tty Mom's Razor: Mom + asleep = cookies and cartoons.

* CHAPTER 10 *

It Only Takes a Partial Village if You Just Have One Kid

People get annoyed if you stop at one child. They say you're self-ish for not giving your kid a sibling, that your kid could turn out spoiled and awkward. These people are usually called "grand-parents." Beware the grandparent! They are a vengeful folk who enjoy the schadenfreude of watching their grandchild inflict on you the same pain that you inflicted on them. And they want more of it.

The other second-child evangelists are friends who've just had their second child. They are desperate for someone else to sit at their two-kids table, and they're jealous that you only semi-ruined your life. They look at the wreckage of your present and want you to bulldoze what's left of it with another kid.

And they will lie.

"The kids play together!"
Yeah? Well, that sure looks like fighting to me.

"We're trying for a third!"
No they're not—the husband just had a vasectomy. And the second kid was an accident.

"We finally feel like a real family!"
Uh, thanks?

Don't fall for it.

ONE CHILD IS DOABLE.

One kid can be chased after, overpowered, and subdued. One child can be pawned off on a relative, taken to a movie, or hidden under a desk in the office at work. One child will play by herself, quietly. You can nap on the weekends with one child (and a locked front door). Just one child to dress in the morning means you won't be too late for most things. You are agile and portable.

You can bring one child to Paris. You won't, but you can.

YOU CAN'T AFFORD IT.

Only two kinds of people have big families: the very poor and the very rich. The poor have limited access to birth control, while the rich have unlimited access to IVF and surrogates. You probably aren't either.

THINK BIG PICTURE.

You can spend the entire college fund on your one kid, instead of splitting it among three kids. And remember that, in the future, you will be an old person who needs help. One grateful Harvard grad will put you in a four-star nursing home, near her house. Three pissed-off community college dropouts will shove you out on the streets.

Your choice.

SIBLINGS SUCK.

How is it that siblings have such a great reputation? Has everyone forgotten how awful brothers and sisters are? They hid your toys, borrowed your Walkman/iPod but then never returned it, told Mom that it was you who drank Dad's bourbon and wore your favorite blouse without asking. Even now they will mention at the Thanksgiving table that this is your fourth boyfriend-free holiday in a row, and insinuated that your kid isn't as verbal as theirs.

Oh, and one of them keeps putting your seventh-grade class picture on Facebook. Who needs these people?

THE WRONG SIBLING CAN RUIN YOUR CHILD'S LIFE.

Just ask David Dahmer. Well, you can't. He changed his last name and went underground after his brother got busted for eating people. As did Paula Hitler, sister to Adolf. Oh, how quickly the "brother who played with me" becomes the "maniac I was never close to."

Conversely, what if there was a smart, talented Kardashian sister? A strange sibling to Kim, Khloe, and Kourtney, born with a high IQ and the capacity for shame. A Kardashian who had sex off-camera and worried about doing something meaningful with her life. A Kardashian with the kapacity to komprehend kalculus, khemistry, or psykhology. Imagine the wretched loneliness of such a kreature. Perhaps this kursed Kardashian exists and, like Paula Hitler or David Dahmer before her, she saw the irreparable damage done to her surname and changed it. Maybe she lives among us. A kollege graduate enjoying a kuiet life in the kountry.

DON'T GET COCKY.

It's OK to quit while you're ahead. Just because you had one great kid doesn't mean that the next one will be worthwhile. You aren't special because you made a good one, you're lucky. Imagine if the Baldwins had stopped after Alec, or the Sheens after Emilio.

Remember: One kid is a carry-on bag—portable and manageable. Two or more is checked luggage—costly and likely to get lost.

CHAPTER 11

How to Leave Your Baby in the Car While You Dash into a 7-Eleven

Some actions that ought be legal are not. Smoking pot, selling sex, and murdering an ex for not paying child support are but three. And while it's not "illegal-illegal" to run into a convenience store to pay for gas while your baby stays in the car, it certainly doesn't *feel* legal. At the very least, it's frowned upon.

It shouldn't be.

Before we continue, let's pause for a moment and consider those poor parents who have forgotten their babies in their car, only to return ten hours later to find that the worst has happened. This is truly awful, and they have our empathy. Most important: It's not their fault. The real problem here is that babies do not know when to cry. It would behoove them to learn.

How is it that babies can scream through the night but when you're about to leave them in the hot car, not a peep? Do they even want to live? Why hasn't the evolutionary process hard-wired an "I'M IN THE BACKSEAT" scream into all babies' DNA? It is a glaring omission that completely undermines Darwin's credibility.

Plus, the only reason these parents forget their baby is that they're in a fugue state thanks to three A.M. feedings of the afore-mentioned baby. Let's face it, babies work against themselves and, like Democrats, are often their own worst enemies.

Unfortunately, the desire to prevent more tragedy has dis-couraged moms from engaging in the very practical habit of leaving one's baby in the car for two freaking minutes.

WHY IT'S OK.

To paraphrase Hobbes, running errands with a baby is nasty, brutish, and long. The smallest activities take forever. Each time you exit the vehicle, you have to open the back car door, unbuckle a five-point buckle that would drive even Rubik mad, and pull the baby out. You probably had to wake him up, too. (That's the real crime.) Now your cranky, just-woken-up baby goes in either a stroller or a sling.

The stroller has to be removed from the trunk, unfolded, and popped open. One of the metal levers will stick—every time. The stroller's hippie cousin, the wrap, comes with ropes, pulleys, and a useless instructional video. If you do succeed in securing your baby into your wrap, don't get excited. You will never be able to replicate that sequence of events. Each time will be as frustrating as the first.

Then, when you're done grocery shopping, the stroller must be folded up, the wrap unspooled, and the baby buckled back in to the car seat. Now it's time to go to the post office.

And repeat.

Any instance when you can eliminate this brain-deadening process, do. Even just two minutes of convenience feels like a reprieve. This baby is strapped to you constantly. You are allowed to dart away for a quick cup of to-go coffee and dart back. It will save time and, for a few moments, you will feel light again.

How can you do it?

HIDE THE BABY. NOT FROM PREDATORS, BUT FROM DO-GOODERS.

Do-gooders are actually more prevalent than pedophiles. In fact, they deserve their own registry. When you move to a new area, the police should have to tell you how many people in your neighborhood have unnecessarily called CPS. Luckily, at least one-third of all people loitering outside a 7-Eleven are wanted for a felony. They don't want the cops stopping by any more than you do.

COVER THE BABY WITH A BLANKET.

Michael Jackson did it all the time. (By the way, this is the only parenting technique Sh*tty Mom will steal from him.) Now the sleeping baby looks like a load of laundry.

DON'T LEAVE YOUR KEYS IN THE IGNITION.

Oh sure: You live in the Midwest and that's how you do things in Minnesota.

You are begging to have your car stolen. Stop being selfish and think for a second about this poor carjacker. All he wants is some wheels. He doesn't want your baby. He can't even afford to pay for his own babies—that's why he's stealing your car in the first place. He came to this 7-Eleven for a Slurpee and someone else's car, and now he's looking at kidnapping charges. That's a potential death penalty case. Nobody wants that.

 Remember: You are dashing into a convenience store, not checking out reference books at the New York Public Library. This is a three-minute operation, tops.

Never Wake Up a Sleeping Baby

This is one of the oldest parenting axioms, and it should apply to more than just babies. Let's face it, the only time people of all ages are tolerable is when they are asleep. They can't make demands, point out flaws, or act on their worst desires. When he was asleep, Cambodian dictator Pol Pot didn't look like the kind of guy who executed people for wearing glasses. In fact, he probably looked like a cute little baby.

Riding in the car puts your infant to sleep. Taking her out of the car wakes her up. That is the only thing you tell the police when they arrest you. A woken-up baby speaks for herself, and if your lawyer can't use that argument to get the abandonment charges dropped, he should be disbarred.

CHAPTER 12

Organized Sports Might Be Great for the Kids, but They Suck for You

Like whooping cough, organized sports are highly contagious. You can vaccinate against them by not signing up the two-year-old for soccer classes. (If we can agree that the two-year-old at soccer practice is a two-year-old running on a field, then we can agree that the same thing can be accomplished by driving the two-year-old to any old field, and at your convenience.)

Eventually, your kids will come in contact with other kids who swim, run, or play base/foot/soft/basketball. And they'll want to join the team, too.

Uniforms. Equipment. Early mornings. Other parents. Goddamnit.

Look, you can't completely slack off on extracurricular activities. Remember, you're not just raising a child, you're raising a person who may one day be granted power of attorney over your finances.

You need her to have a few fond memories of her childhood.

But beware of organized sports: The governing bodies will seduce your young child with colorful participant ribbons and shiny competitor trophies. Before long, your daughter will be obsessed. There are only three possible outcomes to this scenario and they're all horrible.

YOUR KID IS NOT A TALENTED ATHLETE.
Sucking feels shitty, and at some point, your kid will want to quit. At this point, you'll have to decide which coffee mug platitude to teach: the John Wooden standby, "Quitters never win and win-

ners never quit," or the easier to implement "Cut your losses." Try to conceal your ecstasy that the eight A.M. T-ball games may be coming to an end.

YOUR KID IS AN AVERAGE ATHLETE.

She gets third place just enough times to make her think first place is within reach. If this keeps up into her teenage years, you'll be putting in the same hours and expenses as an Olympian's mom, but with no scholarship to make it all worthwhile. For every "Michael Phelps's Mom" there are a hundred "For Ten Years, I Sat on the Bleachers Next to Michael Phelps's Mom" moms.

YOUR KID IS AN EXCEPTIONAL ATHLETE.

Even worse, your kid could be talented. That's the end of family dinners and summer vacations. Casually mention your family's trip to the Grand Canyon at a swim meet, and two hours later the swim coach is at your house, wild-eyed. The league championships are held over Labor Day weekend, and your daughter is the backstroke leg of the medley relay.

At the high school level, committing to a time-intensive sport doesn't allow your teenager to have a normal childhood. Three- or four-hour workouts each day means that she'll miss out on classic American experiences like getting a job at McDonald's, getting high before going to the job at McDonald's, and getting fired for being high while on the job at McDonald's.

MAKING ATHLETES THE MICHAEL LANDON WAY.

The Loneliest Runner was a semiautobiographical 1970s made-for-TV movie written by Michael Landon about a teenage boy who was a chronic bed wetter. To shame him into stopping, his mother would hang his pee-stained sheets outside the window. Every day, the boy would run home to yank the sheets down before any of his friends saw them. Eventually, these daily pee-sheet wind sprints led to the boy becoming a track star and an Olympic gold medalist.

Is it true? No. But just because it's fiction doesn't mean that, in our overstructured era, you can't long for the days when terrible parenting created a great athlete.

 Remember: Some moms make athletes, Sh*tty Moms make fans. Somebody's got to yell at the TV on Super Bowl Sunday.

CHAPTER 13

How to Feel Nothing When You Dump Them at Grandma's for the Weekend/Week/Month/Summer/Ever

It should be an easy decision. Your baby is exhausting you, and your mom or mother-in-law wants to help. She's offered to take care of your baby for as long as you need. A night. A weekend. Whatever you want, honey! You can sleep late... take a shower, uninterrupted... have a date night.

And yet, you can't.

You have worked so hard for this baby. You suffered through some miscarriages, or you IVFed five times before the egg finally took, or you flew to China and adopted, or you gave up on IVF, decided to adopt, bought a plane ticket to China, and then got pregnant. The point is, your baby is finally here, totally yours, and you feel compelled to spend every possible moment with her.

You don't know it yet, but you've lost your mind.

BABIES WERE DESIGNED TO BE PASSED OFF TO STRANGERS.

A baby is chubby, cute, and helpless. That is precisely so someone will take her from you for five minutes. You've become like the hoarder who can't see that her house is full of mice. You need a reality show to unhinge the baby from your arms. Give her to grandma and draw yourself a nice, hot Epsom salt bath.

YOU ARE NO PRIZE.

Good God woman, look at yourself. Or better yet, rent *Sweeney*

Todd and check out Helena Bonham Carter. Cause that's you. Ratty hair, crazy eyes, making questionable food choices. Now think of your poor baby. She spends all day staring at you, wondering if this is how she's going to look when she grows up. Of course she is crying.

Your baby needs to see how rested adults behave. If she goes only by you, she'll think it's normal to shout, "I can't do this anymore!" and storm out of the house to sit in the car and eat cheese.

Knowing you aren't the only kind of person on Earth gives your baby a ray of hope.

OLD PEOPLE HAVE SOMETHING TO CONTRIBUTE.

Grandparents possess a unique wisdom that comes from being near death. They remember wars, cheap coffee, and your "asshole phase" that started at around age fourteen and hasn't quite ended. Your mother is eager to share her knowledge, and since you stopped listening to her the day she said you could stand to lose a few pounds, your baby is all she has left. And after being disappointed in you, her expectations are more reasonable. Whatever she did to you will be diluted considerably by the passage of time and arthritis.

GRANDCHILDREN ARE A DO-OVER.

Unfortunately, your mother can't go back in time and not grab your back fat when you tried on a bikini. That, along with your sister being "the talented one," is in the books, forever. But your baby is a blank canvas—she's you, minus the resentment and the memory. And your mom has about thirty years' worth of emotional paint that's about to dry out.

 Remember: You look like hell. Get some sleep and wash your hair.

Things to Do in Your Own Home While You're the Only One in It

OK, the baby is gone. You have four days. You may assume you're supposed to go to a spa or spend lots of money. Well, sure. But for one of those days, Sh*tty Mom prescribes the following: Lead your exact same life, but without the baby and/or kids.

You won't appreciate how much your kids have altered your life until you blaze through a to-do list, by yourself.

Take a shower.
A long one, with the bathroom door closed. Oooh, look! There's shampoo in the bottle because your kid didn't dump it out all at once so that she could make a bubble mountain.

Go grocery shopping.
It's amazing how quickly you can buy everything you need when you aren't telling the five-year-old to stop licking the apples, or asking the seven-year-old to find his brother, who you last saw running down the cereal aisle. Take time to look at foreign cheeses, organic spices, and fruit hybrids. Look how quickly you can morph from tired mom into pretentious foodie. Brooklyn, here you come!

Walk to the park.
The same one you take your kid to. But now you can be that strange lady on the bench who reads books without looking up every minute to scan the sandbox. See those moms in high-waist jeans, tennis shoes, and sweatshirts? Most days, that's what everyone sees when they look at you.

Sobering.

Walk home at an adult's pace, without carrying a tired three-year-old in one arm and pushing her tricycle with the other. So light, so breezy. This must be the reason people enjoy taking walks.

Make dinner.

Sit where you usually sit, and eat the entire meal, by yourself. How does it feel to keep all the good bites for yourself, no sharing? No insisting that the vegetables be eaten . . . no making threats that you don't have the energy to enforce. Just chew, swallow, and relax.

Now you're ready to party like the wild, single woman that you are for the next six hours. Pull the childproof covers off the electrical outlets. You can do it—there's nobody in the house who wants to stick a wet finger in there. Then, go to the kitchen, take out a knife and . . . leave it out on the counter . . . within the reach of a child . . . so unsafe, and so close to the bleach that you didn't put up on a high shelf.

Hell, yeah. You wild girl, you still got it.

CHAPTER 14

Free Gear: Get It from Your Selfish Friends

The three biggest wastes of a new mom's money are new clothes, new baby furniture, and every single toy.

CLOTHES.
Admit it, the outfits are for you, not the baby. No judgment—dressing a baby in coordinated clothes is inexplicably satisfying. They do look cute. But toddlers are like grandfathers—they don't give a damn if their clothes match.

FURNITURE.
C'mon. Who are you impressing with the Bellini nursery set? Your single friends can't tell a new crib from a large UPS box, and your mom friends will praise your taste to your face while silently thinking you're a rich jerk.

Don't be fooled by furniture ads with the lovestruck new mom breastfeeding her newborn in a mahogany rocking chair in a peaceful, green nursery room. That will happen exactly twice—then Operation Breastfeed will move into the family room, or wherever you keep the big-screen TV and the comfy couch.

TOYS.
You can't predict what your kid will play with. The Melissa & Doug farm animal puzzle will go unsolved while your kid snaps rubber bands for two weeks.

You need to get all of this shit in the form of hand-me-downs. In olden times, moms were generous with their old clothes. But now, thanks to fertility drugs and certain celebrities, everyone thinks they can have twins when they're forty-five. Women knee-deep in perimenopause are holding on to all of it... just in case.

So, what do you do if you see a toy or a doll or a jacket that your friend's child is no longer using?

1. **Take it.** If she's like 99 percent of the moms, she won't notice it's gone. If she does, she'll think it's somewhere in the garage or that her husband lost it. Obviously, your kid can't wear it or play with it in her presence, so be an organized thief and keep track of your stash on an Excel spreadsheet. Of course, this only applies to items that her kids have outgrown (according to you). You can always sneak it back into her house when your child ages up.

2. **Borrow it.** This is the same as taking it, except you're doing it with her blessing. You both know that you aren't returning the train station roundabout. In fact, you'll probably lend it to another friend, and so on and so forth, until it falls apart. Then its final owner will donate it to Goodwill and write it off at its original price.

3. **Ask for it.** But only if you don't have the balls to take it. If she says no, you are screwed. You have tipped your hand. She has something you covet. She will notice when it's missing, suspect you instantly, and never invite you over again. And then how will you get your hands on that Emily train?

Unfortunately, asking is the only way to get furniture. Unless you are the kind of person who can smuggle a changing table in your purse. Then *you* should've written this book.

 Remember: The Velveteen Rabbit only became Real after he was used up by a Boy. You aren't stealing, you are making things more Real.

Hey, How Do I Get Rid of All This Crap?

Your child has accumulated too many toys. He doesn't agree with this opinion. In fact, he believes that every toy is necessary. Especially if he hasn't played with it in nine months and forgot about it until he saw you throwing it away. Those toys are most important.

Now you must use the skills you honed while building your toy chest. Take a toy and hide it. If your kid doesn't ask for it within a week, he has forgotten about it. It is tossable. Do this once per week until you have a sizeable stash, something worth the trip to a Salvation Army or a church. (Of course, you can't give it to anyone your kid will see at a playdate.)

If you are in search of a "teachable" moment, tell your child that he is going to donate his toys to poor kids. When you explain that some little boys have *no* trains, your son may tap into some newfound empathy and be happy to share his fourth Thomas the Tank Engine with someone less fortunate. Or he may decide that poor people are assholes who take his stuff. Be careful, you are shaping the political thought of a generation.

CHAPTER 15

This Tradition Must Die:
Handwritten Thank-you Notes

There is no greater waste of time in the final months of your pregnancy than the writing of thank-you notes. Instead of enjoying your life's final eight-hour stretches of sleep, you're looking for stamps, picking out cards, and remembering how to write in cursive. You're trying to match gifts to givers—and you're down to the last two friends. One gave you a box of Huggies, and the other, bedding from Pottery Barn Kids, and you can't remember who gave what.

Factor in the energy-suck that comes from months of procrastination, and you will regret ever getting pregnant in the first place.

DON'T EXPECT YOURSELF TO WRITE THEM, AND DON'T FEEL GUILTY.

The minute you open a gift, thank your friend profusely in person. Tell her that she will go unthanked in print. That is your gift to her, because receiving a thank-you note is almost as torturous as writing one.

How long are you supposed to keep someone's thank-you note? A week, a year? Until you feel thanked? Where does one keep it? In the living room, on an end table, next to that figurine that gives you the creeps, or on the refrigerator, beside the Ambien prescription? Or should you keep it forever, in hopes that its sender is implicated in a sex scandal, or wins *American Idol*? It's too much to worry about.

Furthermore, the thank-you note is a class divider. In an

era when an e-mail would suffice, the author of a thank-you note reminds her recipient that she has time on her hands and a nanny to pick up the kids. She's not ending her days in an exhausted heap, watching *Friends* reruns and falling asleep with her makeup still on. Thank-you notes are the modern-day equivalent of pale skin and uncalloused hands.

This tradition must end.

 Remember: It starts with you. Do your part by doing nothing.

The Journey of a Holiday Card with a Photo of the Giver's Children on the Cover

* Open a card from your friend Sarah.
* See that the cover is a photo of Sarah's kids, in holiday outfits.
* Realize that Sarah has dressed up her kids, hired a photographer, taken pictures, selected one, had it printed, and then addressed, stamped, and mailed each envelope so that the card would arrive before the holidays.
* Remember that you totally fucking forgot to do that.
* Wait—you put your daughter's picture on a Christmas card a few years ago. You have some leftovers in the garage—maybe you can send one to Sarah?
* Whoops. Your daughter was a one-year-old when those cards were made, now she is nine. Never mind.
* Place Sarah's card on your fridge.
* Put two photos of your daughter on the fridge, so the refrigerator photos of your family outnumber Sarah's 2:1.
* Invite Sarah over for coffee, so she can see her card on your fridge.
* Throw it away.

CHAPTER 16

How to Leave Your Kids to Go on a Business Trip

After you have kids, business trips suck. In addition to packing your things, you have to sort out theirs. Sitters are arranged, grandmothers are flown in, phone numbers are written down, clothes are washed and folded, car pools are covered, and food is prepared. You are a warden leaving inmates in the care of a substitute.

If you're heading out of town, it must be important.

In this moment, as you try to make up for your absence, you are vulnerable to guilt. And your kids know it. It's probably some evolutionary crap, with babies doing whatever they could to convince their mothers not to leave them, vulnerable to a dingo attack. But we don't live in huts or squat in caves. We have mortgages, and we pay them with jobs that might require travel.

Do kids care? No. If kids had their way, you would quit your job and the gym and hang out with them all day, eating Goldfish.

As you zip your suitcase closed, they are doing anything to make you stay. Cute and cuddly one moment, hysterical the next. Children truly are shape-shifters, deserving of their own show on HBO. When the cab pulls up, your kids will say horrible things like "Don't leave, Mama, we love you."

DO AS MUCH BUSINESS AS POSSIBLE WHEN THEY ARE INFANTS.

Contrary to popular wisdom, a baby's first year is when you should double down on the hard work. Make partner, go to conventions—shove it all in before he can ask you to stay home.

YOU ARE NOT SPECIAL.

When your kid says, "I love you," she means it as much as she did yesterday, when she said it to an Elmo doll.

THEY HAVE AN AGENDA.

Kids know that guilt, like Santa Claus, brings gifts. When you feel like a Sh*tty Mom, they get a present. It is in their best interest to make you feel terrible.

THEY ARE DISLOYAL TO A FAULT.

Within five minutes of your departure, Dad will give them ice cream and they'll be like, "Mom who?"

DAD IS THEIR FAVORITE.

Unless their father is the Great Santini, a week alone with Dad is spring break for kids. It's a vacation from brushing their teeth and taking baths. It's M&M's for breakfast, frosting for lunch, and sugar cubes for dinner. And a ten P.M. bedtime.

AND YOU AREN'T EVEN NUMBER TWO.

Not only does Dad occupy first place in their hearts, but second place goes to anyone who lets them watch TV. As you sob in your hotel room, unable to enjoy quiet and solitude, your kid is telling the babysitter that she's prettier than Mom.

Remember: The only thing they'll say when you get home is "What did you get me?" In the end, it's all about the airport snow globe.

Things You Should Do in a Different City Before You Go Home

It doesn't matter where you are—London, Tokyo, or Cincinnati. It only matters where you aren't: with the kids. Stop checking in, stop Skyping. They're fine, and your freedom will end soon. If you have even a few hours to yourself, try doing one or all of these things:

Browse.

How long has it been since you've gone to a bookstore and headed directly to the fiction aisle? Then stayed there, for twenty minutes? Without wondering where your kid went, or sitting through Storytime, or spending $10 on a children's book that has forty words in it, total. How long has it been since you read a book where the protagonist is a person, not a monkey or a dog or a tugboat? Be an optimist. Buy a book. Promise yourself you will finish it this year.

You know you want to . . .

After you finish feeding your brain, make time to visit a female-friendly sex-toy shop. Buy a vibrator—let that ole vag of yours relive her glory days. C'mon, what else are you going to do in your hotel room tonight?

See an independent movie.

It's not enough to see an R-rated movie at a mall movie chain—you'll run into kids there. This business trip is your vacation, it should be completely child-free. Go to one of those snotty independent movie houses that only show foreign films or American ones starring Maggie Gyllenhaal. Feels good to be a grown-up again, doesn't it?

A bar.

Sh*tty Mom hesitates to bring this up, because if you're the kind of person who needs to be reminded to drink alcohol, perhaps alcohol isn't for you. But if your hotel has a bar, or you're in a city with cabs . . . there's no reason you can't get yourself buzzed before you take yourself back to your room and put batteries in the vibrator.

OTHER PEOPLE ARE HORRIBLE

CHAPTER 17

Someone Stole Your Baby Name! aka Ballad of the First Aidan Mom

"I hope you don't mind, but we were thinking of naming our baby [your child's name]."

Imagine the plight of the mom who, pregnant with a boy in 2000, bravely decided to bring back the name Aidan (or Aiden). It wasn't popular back then, and no one but the most fervent Aidan Quinn fan was even aware of it. A great name, a nugget of gold picked from a riverbed filled with the same twelve apostles' names.

And how was this mom rewarded for her vision? By copycats, who nudged Aidan into the Social Security's Top 100 list of boys' names and then into the Top 10. Not to mention the creative spellings (Aaden, Aidyn) and the rhymes (Braedon, Caydon, and Jayden). Finally, in December of 2009, BabyCenter.com declared it the top boy's name of the decade.

Aidan Mom had to wonder: Could she have done anything to stop it?

Don't let that happen to you.

Look, you did all the legwork. You pored over books and websites, in search of a name that would prophesy greatness. You became an expert in Greek and Latin root words. Your first choice for a girl, "Sophia," is Greek and means "wisdom," and you deftly used that fact to shoot down your husband's first choice, "Darcy," which is French and means... "from Arcy."

If you are an immigrant, you wondered if you should keep it ethnically real with "Liu Liu," or go full-throttle all-American with "Jennifer." Fit in, or stand out? If you are white, you convinced yourself that one Irish great-grandparent justifies naming your son "Declan" and your daughter "Maeve."

You read *Freakonomics* and prudently avoided the middle name "Wayne." In short, you researched, you argued, and, finally, you decided. And then some bitch comes along and steals your baby's name.

If her baby is still in utero:

> **Speak up!** In today's world, there is no reason for any preschool to have more than one Holden (certain parts of Manhattan excepted). Remind your friend that this is the twenty-first century. Any noun can be a name. A fruit, a city, an IKEA product (when will their "Vika" line crack the girls' Top 10?).

> **Provide substitutes.** You can't take "Maude" away from her without providing some imaginative alternates. Suggest one of your backup names. You and she obviously have the same taste, and c'mon, you aren't having another kid. Let your friend have "Audrey." (If your birth control fails, you still have "Caroline" in your back pocket.)

If her baby has been born:

> **End the friendship.** What else is this bitch going to take from you? Your job? Your husband?
> "Caroline"?

 Remember: If you don't say anything, your daughter "Stella" will instead be known as "Olivia C. The blond Olivia C."

How to Tell When Your Friends Are Pretending They Like Your Baby's Name

You went your own way with the baby's name. You picked a name that you're pretty sure no one else will touch. You like it, your husband likes it, and that's all that matters. Besides, if first names were destiny, Condoleezza Rice would have been a stripper.

Back to your friend. Perhaps she is old-fashioned—raised to be a Jacob Mom or an Emily Mom. Your name has taken her by surprise.

She will ask you to spell it. This is a stalling technique. She really wants to say, "Uh, what the fuck did you just say?" Spellcheck is a gentle way for her to confirm that, yes, your son's name is Z-e-p-h-y-r.

She may ask, "How did you come up with that?" She is giving you the benefit of the doubt. Maybe it was a family name. In fact, before you answer, she'll suggest that very thing, and her voice will trail upwards: "Sounds like a family name . . . ?"

Your response, "It is, now," will not help her.

CHAPTER 18

Unspeakable Evil: Private Birthday Party—with a Bouncy Castle—at a Public Park

There is a special place in hell for parents who have their kid's birthday party in a public park *and* rent a bouncy castle. (And that hell is a never-ending kid's birthday party with two bouncy castles.) Unknowing moms and dads amble up to the park for a relaxing afternoon of texting and judging. Instead, they're treated to endless whines from their children: "I want to play in the bouncy castle!"

Their kids' tear-streaked faces pressed up against a giant plastic bubble.

How is a Sh*tty Mom like you supposed to keep her child from trying to crash a bouncy-castle party?

1. Don't.

Talking your way into a place where you're not wanted is a survival skill, and your number-one job as a parent is to teach your child how to survive. Look, Earth is doomed. One day, a meteor will hit the planet or a nuclear bomb will hit the country. So back off and let your kid take his best shot. The four-year-old who can fudge his way into a private bouncy castle will grow into the man who can talk his way into a locked fallout shelter. Or at least into a packed restaurant that won't seat without a reservation.

This is bigger than you or this other kid's birthday party.

2. Play dumb.

* Keep a low profile until your kid gets busted. It's best not to outwardly condone grifty behavior.
* Shift the blame. After the exasperated bouncy mom yells, "Hey, whose kid is this," spring up from your bench and shout, "Hey, what the hell are you doing with my kid?"

3. Leave the park.

Your kid will probably be upset, and who can blame him? It truly is not fair. Greet him like Paulie did a young Henry Hill in *Goodfellas*, after his first pinch outside the courthouse. Give your kid a hug and tell him you're proud because he broke his cherry (don't explain what that means just yet). Then take him out for some ice cream.

 Remember: It's never too early to start resenting the kind-of-rich kids.

CHAPTER 19

Put a Stop to the Awful Nickname Your Father-in-Law Gave Your Kid

Imagine the chill that soars up the spine of an Isabella Mom the first time her daughter is called "Izzy." Mom nervously tries to steer the *Titanic* back toward "Isabella" or at least "Bella," but it's too late. The "Izzy" iceberg has been struck. Now, it's fifteen years of "Can Izzy come out to play?" and "Is Izzy home?" Which will itself be shortened to "Is-zy home?"

Don't be surprised if the daughter named for Spain's greatest queen will hook up with a Charles and, together, they will be "Chuck and Izzy."

NEVER SHORTEN YOUR CHILD'S NAME, NOT EVEN ONCE.

It's the start of a slippery slope. If friends, family, or neighbors hear you call your Margaret "Meg," they will take matters into their own hands and, before you know it, you're the proud mother of a "Marge." People are jerks that way.

MAKE YOUR FEELINGS KNOWN.

It doesn't matter who the nicknamer is—devoted uncle, well-meaning grandpa. As Henry's mom, you've got to get the word out that "Hank" is unacceptable. Slash their tires, key your child's full name into their car. It's send-a-message time.

STAY AWAY FROM THE CLASSICS.

People like to tamper with great names. Is it jealousy? It must be. How else does Maureen become "Mo" or Elizabeth "Betsy"? Maybe that's why made-up names are popular. Once you put in the effort to crack the spelling and pronunciation of "Nevaeh" (it's "Heaven" spelled backward, and it was the twenty-fifth most popular girl's name in 2010), you don't want to void all of your hard work by calling the kid "Nev."

Remember: Nicknames should never be derived from first names. Instead, nicknames should be cruel reminders of your child's physical flaws, like "Brace Face" and "Four Eyes" and "Fatso."

AND SOMETIMES THE ASSHOLE IS YOU

* CHAPTER 20 *

How to Drop Off Your Sick Kid at Daycare Before the Teacher Figures It Out

If you read that title and thought, *Oh, I could never do that! It's so irresponsible! Just stay home!*, then this chapter is not for you. Move along, princess. Enjoy your supportive husband or your family nearby or your boss that lets you work from home, or your own money, or whatever it is you have that allows you to react to a working mom's dilemma with such horror.

Bye-bye.

Is she gone? Good. It's time to discuss the only parenting topic more taboo than incest: taking your sick kid to daycare.

Let's set the table properly so all concerned can understand what's at stake: You have a job. You can't stay home to care for your daughter, and no one else is available either. Yes, you are aware that if you bring her to daycare, she's going to get another kid sick. Well, you can't think about that right now. Eyes on the prize: You have a job.

For now.

If you lose your job because you stayed home with your sick kid, terrible things will happen. You will fall back on your rent or mortgage, and you will be evicted. You and your child(ren) will be thrown onto the streets, in this economy. To pay for the seedy hotel that you now call home, you will sell your body. You will strut all over your corner (yes, you will secure a corner) and lean into car windows. You will negotiate the price of a blow job. And sister, they go for a lot less than they should.

And where are the kids during all this debauchery? If you couldn't leave them home alone when you had a good job, you certainly can't do it now. The kids are in your car, counting your money. For now, they don't know how you earn it. All they know is: Mommy goes for a ride, then Mommy brings back $35. Ten or twenty times a day. "Well," you tell yourself, "at least they're getting good at math."

OK, this may not be exactly how things play out, but it's what you have to tell yourself to stay focused.

THE NUTS AND BOLTS OF A SICK KID DAYCARE DROP-OFF

1. Never bring your kid to school if she has a fever.
2. Correction: Never bring your kid to daycare if you *know* she has a fever, which is why you should never take your child's temperature, especially if she feels hot. The less you know, the less you have to lie about.
3. Teachers can tell when you're lying. Like cops, they hear the same bullshit over and over again. If the teacher asks point-blank if your daughter has a fever, you can't say no when the answer is yes without tipping her off. However, you *can* look her in the eyes and say, "Not that I know of." Because it's true. Information is your enemy.
4. Drop her off during a busy time, like eight A.M. Get lost in the herd of moms dropping off their healthy-for-now kids. Then run. Try to be in your car before your kid coughs.
5. Teach your child how to cough into her elbow. The less your kid coughs on others, the less likely the teacher is to call you at work.
6. Teach her how to say, "I have allergies." If she's particularly articulate: "year-round allergies."
7. If the teacher does call you at work, don't pick up the

phone. Better yet, leave the phone in the car. How can you feel guilty about missing a call if you don't have your phone with you? Remember: Information is your enemy.

8. Don't return a call from daycare until the second voice mail. If your kid is *really* sick, they will leave multiple messages.

9. If you have to pick up your kid, wait until the end of the day. Pick her up an hour earlier than normal. You'll still get there before closing time, but you won't be leaving work too early.

10. You work when you're sick—most people do. It's the new America. And how can we compete in a global economy if our kids stay home every time they have a "cold" or "strep throat"? Take your sick kid to daycare. For yourself. For America.

 Remember: Your kid got sick from some other Sh*tty Mom's sick kid. Why should you be a hero and stop the virus in its tracks? Pay it forward.

What a Sh*tty Mom's Mom, a Retired Preschool Teacher, Said After Reading This Chapter

"This is a joke, right?"

. . .

"What do you mean you've 'done this' before?"

. . .

"Is that why my granddaughter could cough into her elbow before she could walk? So she wouldn't attract the attention of the teacher when she had a cold?"

. . .

"Well, I'm shocked. I raised you better than that."

. . .

"Yes I did."

. . .

"I tell you what, if you'd been a mom at *my* school, I would've asked you to leave."

. . .

"And another thing: Are you wearing enough sunscreen? Your skin looks terrible."

. . .

"Where are you going? What did I say?"

* CHAPTER 21 *

Should You Stop Texting if Another Mom Yells at Your Kid?

You and your child are at the pirate ship park, tucked away in a gated area. Which means you can text your friend without checking your son's whereabouts every fifteen seconds. You're getting consistent LOLs and the occasional OMG—a relaxing, fun textversation. It's the little things that make life worth living (ITLTTMLWL).

You hear wails, but not your kid's. You continue to text.

You hear wails again, but this time, it's your kid. You stop texting. Your son is standing on the pirate ship. He's crying the tears of a guilty man who fears the jury will convict. You didn't witness the crime, but another three-year-old is rubbing sand from his eyes.

"That wasn't very nice," the vic's mom says to your son. She is wagging her finger in his face.

"Waaaah," your son cries, looking for you.

Don't put that phone down just yet.

Let's pause and assess. Is your kid being a jerk? He is descended from you, and you're reading a book called *Sh*tty Mom*, so it's possible you have a shitty kid. In fact, it's probable. All kids are assholes some times—maybe today is your boy's day. Only rookies assume their kid is innocent. If yours threw sand, he needs to be disciplined. In your absence, this mom has stepped in.

Let her. You need a day off from lecturing, and she has apparently brought her "A" game. Settle in on the bench and watch the show. A couple things could happen:

* **You can observe your child's lying technique from afar.** So this is what he's like at preschool. He looks at his feet when he lies to a stranger. Good to know.

* **You are the devil your child knows.** Another mom's parenting style may help your kid appreciate yours. Finally.

* **You realize she is better at resolving conflict, and steal her technique.**

* **You realize you are better at resolving conflict.** Every now and then, it's good to acknowledge that you aren't the shittiest Sh*tty Mom.

Get off the bench if:

* **The mom hits your kid.** Whoa. That's your gig.

But wait. What if *you're* the mom stuck disciplining someone else's ill-mannered kid?

Well, that's a different matter altogether. At the end of the day, Sh*tty Mom is Team Reader. If you're that other mom, then so are we. Here goes.

Sister, you didn't buckle your baby in the car, fill the sippy cups, and drive to the park so you could teach Empathy 101 to some disengaged layabout's unattended kid. How dare she plop her fat ass on a bench, sexting last night's booty call, all the while pretending she's not responsible for the brat who threw sand in your kid's eyes?

* **Speak to her child in a voice that's loud enough for her to hear.** If she doesn't come right away, you are being used. (She might have read this book. . . . Sorry.)

* **Make her kid rat her out.** Call her over. It's hands-on-hips time. Then mean mug her until she forces her kid to apologize. You didn't watch all five seasons of *The Wire* for nothing.

Don't worry if you aren't active in the park. Every mom has an age she rocks, and maybe you aren't a "toddler mom." If you want to talk politics or girls or boys or music with your kid, you're probably more of a "teenager mom." You could even be an "after they leave for college mom." You never know when you will blossom.

> **Remember:** She thinks you're lazy. You think she's a helicopter. Hey, you're both right!

CHAPTER 22

How to Hand Off the Newborn Who Just Filled a Diaper

You carried the baby, then you had the baby. You did the hard emotional and/or physical work. You're home from the hospital, you're beat, and this infant that you are hoping you feel love for soon will just *not* stop crapping.

1. **Learn to recognize the Mother's Window.**
   The Mother's Window is a small window of opportunity that only a mom recognizes. In this case, it's the seconds between the moment your baby has pooped in his diaper and when everyone else smells it. Figuring it out is a crucial part of the bonding process.

   Every baby has his own "Ahhh" face, and when your baby makes his, you have a short amount of time to hand him off to Dad, Grandpa, or the babysitter. Get to know your baby. Let him help you not change his diaper.

2. **Sneak out of the room.**
   Just go. You may hear a protest cry from the adult, but learn the Bible story of Lot's wife: Do not look back. Walk away from that mess like an action star walks away from a deadly explosion. Slowly, with a smirk on your face.

3. **Simply refuse.**
   You are allowed to fall apart. Multiple mini-breakdowns may prevent a big one. It is totally acceptable to say "Your

turn" to whoever is nearby. Save those hands of yours for cradling the baby's head during a feeding.

Remember: The Mother's Window Five-Second Countdown: Baby grunts . . . 5 . . . Baby poops . . . 4 . . . Mom realizes . . . 3 . . . Hands off baby . . . 2 . . . Leaves the room . . . 1 . . . The room is assaulted by smell. Mom is gone.

CHAPTER 23

Oh, You Just Had an Epic Meltdown

As a mom, you've had a good couple weeks. Baths have been given, age-appropriate YouTube videos have been watched, and books have been read.

Something clicked, you're in a groove. You start thinking maybe it's time to add some weight to your pack. A kitchen remodel? A puppy? Another child? It all seems do-able!

Then, on a crisp, cloudless day . . . a rock tumbles down the mountain in the form of a lost shoe. Then another rock and another until it's a mountain-slide. A sock flushed down the toilet, a diaper pulled off in the crib, peanut butter smeared on two walls, that Mickey Mouse cartoon on YouTube turns out to be a porno starring a girl named "Minnie Mouth."

What happens next will become the stuff of family lore. You are about to lose your shit in epic fashion. Fifty years from now, your oldest will recount this day to huge laughs at your wake. Words are screamed, butts are spanked, walls are kicked, a watermelon is smashed. When you finish, everyone is crying— your kids, your husband, your dog, you.

OK.

What should you do?

LOOK ON THE BRIGHT SIDE.

* **Everyone is alive!** (Right?) OK! GOOD. Screaming? Even better . . . They are *super* alive.

* **Are you at a Walmart?** No? GOOD. Yes? Oh no! Get out of Walmart, ASAP. The store's yellow happy face mascots

are staring at you, making your meltdown all that more ironic. (If you must have a meltdown in a store, you will feel less trashy at a Target.)

* **Know that it happens to everyone.** While no one is condoning child abuse, every mother deserves one "Get Out of Family Court Free" card.

If this happens a lot, you can get cheap or free therapy. MFT grads are required to give thousands of hours of supervised therapy before they can get their license. Let a newbie take a crack at you! Your craziness can turn an ordinary grad student into a real therapist.

If it's just a onetime freak-out, you are probably furious with yourself for losing your cool. Instead of beating yourself up for being the mother that you are, take a moment and focus on the mother that you aren't:

Your Own

Correction: Your two-pack-a-day, secondhand smoke-blowing mom. Just spitballing here, but a list of her probable crimes include:

* Putting you in the backseat without a seat belt
* Putting you in the front seat with just a lap belt
* Letting you ride your bike without a helmet
* Allowing you to sell Girl Scout cookies by yourself, in the exclusive Pedophile Woods condominium complex
* Telling you to stand up straight because hunched over you "look pregnant"
* Letting your male swim/gymnastics/track coach take you on overnight trips that included pre-competition "rubdowns"
* Having never heard of bulimia, commenting on your weight loss by saying, "Whatever you're doing, honey, keep it up!"
  That lady is lucky the statute of limitations ran out.

A "Toddlers and Tiaras Mom"

Your four-year-old daughter might be screaming that you are mean, but you know what she isn't doing? Trying to out-whore another four-year-old whose mom taught her to lip-synch to Lil' Kim's "Magic Stick."

That Mom Who Lives Down the Street

That once-in-a-lifetime meltdown you just had? She calls that "Monday." She's writing a book called *Fucking Awful Mom*. Look for it in stores next year.

A Florida Mom

OK, that's a joke. Sort of. Maybe not. Sh*tty Mom is conflicted. Of course, not every mom in Florida is terrible, but recent events suggest that, at this moment in history, every terrible mother is from Florida.

If you are a Florida Mom, what the hell is going on down there? Are you being driven insane by the rest of us driving through your state, looking for Disney World? Or is it the senior citizens? Was it a bad idea for all of America to send their parents to Florida, without also sending psychologists for the rest of Florida? Can you leave Florida, raise your kids in Minnesota, then return when you are of retirement age and too old to do anything but enjoy the Early Bird Special?

A Meth Mom

While there's no "good" time to be a meth addict, certainly the worst time would be when you are pregnant. And you didn't do that. Tiny victories!

A "Not This Time" Mom

Look, you could have avoided this whole mess with one quick trip to Planned Parenthood. (Unless you live in Kansas. Then, it's a twelve-hour bus ride to Chicago.) Instead, you let that damn baby blast a four-lane highway through your quiet, one-way street. Surely that counts for something.

P.S. If you are going to remind your kids that you could have aborted them, save it for the right occasion. That is an ace up your sleeve that you don't want to waste on the three-year-old when she spills her orange juice. Wait until she's fifteen and throws a house party when you're out of town. Sit her down on your beer-soaked couch and explain that you are about to tell her something that she will one day pass on to her own daughter when she trashes her house. Then lean in and say, "I could've gotten rid of you. And I didn't. You're fucking welcome. Now clean up this goddamn mess and never let it happen again or I will build a time machine and take us both back to the day you were conceived."

 Remember: The mom who has never lost control is not worth knowing.

CHAPTER 24

How to Not Hear the Baby in the Middle of the Night

When a mom tells you her baby sleeps through the night, what she's actually telling you is that *she* sleeps through the night. All babies cry through the night. They are self-centered and ill-mannered, and they don't give a shit if they wake you up. Even worse, mothers are hardwired to respond to their baby's cries. There is one way to end this cycle of abuse: Make sure that you are unable to hear your baby cry at night.

1. **The baby should sleep in his own room.**
   It is impossible to ignore your baby when he's crying in a bassinet next to your bed (or even worse, sleeping *in* your bed). He exited your body for a reason—he's ready to move on. Let him.

2. **The baby's room should be nowhere near yours.**
   For God's sake, do not share a wall. Nothing conducts the sound of an infant's wail like drywall. If you live in an apartment, move the crib to the farthest possible wall—preferably one he shares with your neighbor.

3. **Traditional noisemakers don't work.**
   Once you've got the baby as far away as possible, it's time for some aural neutralization. Noise machines are ineffective. Like all animals, babies continue to evolve. Their vocal cords have adapted to modern times and it takes only seconds for their cries to pierce the white noise of

fake crickets, fake birds, fake whales, and fake babbling brooks. Never forget: Babies are crafty, and they are on to us.

4. Buy a fan and leave it on until the baby turns three.
But guess what? Babies have an enemy, and it is the fan. Not the dainty, spinning fan of the 1950s, and not the sophisticated, noiseless fan of the future. No. Babies are unable to fight back against the boxy fan of the '70s. The ugly, cheap fan with a filthy grille. The fan with three settings: "low," "medium," and "I just slept for eight hours and I feel great."

   DO NOT TURN IT OFF. The fan allows you to live in a fantasy world where your baby is a "champion sleeper." But only if it's on. Should you get cocky and flip the setting to "low"? Well, well, well... this is the moment your baby has been waiting for. He knows you are genetically programmed to come to him, and he will open his little mouth and strike your heart with a wail that will destroy your "champion sleeper" illusion.

Remember: As a parent, you will do way more neglectful things than sleep through your baby's cries. This is just the beginning.

OTHER MOMS

CHAPTER 25

Old Moms: Hey, Look Who Had One Good Egg Left!

Congrats old gal, you did it. You had a career, and you had men. Lots and lots of men. Maybe even a woman. You ignored all that "biological clock" crap and partied on, postponing motherhood until the last possible second. And then—when every women's magazine said your forty-four-year-old womb was finished—you cranked out a shorty.

You beat some insane odds.

So, let's take a moment and look back on your accomplished life. You made partner, or headed a division, or became the first female-whatever in your company's history. Or you released eight albums to critical acclaim, or discovered an element, or had groupie sex with a Smashing Pumpkin, or got a second master's degree or a third husband. Your teens, twenties, and thirties are one long blur of doing whatever the fuck you wanted.

Your life was awesome.

And now it's over. Hope you kept diaries. Remember that one decade, where you never woke up before eleven A.M.? It will never happen again—not even when your kid is out of the house. By then, you will be a senior citizen. And guess what old people do? They wake up early. Earlier than babies, earlier than toddlers. They put on velour sweats and powerwalk around the mall.

A few things to keep in mind:

IT'S NO ONE'S BUSINESS HOW YOU GOT PREGNANT.
Did that baby come from your last good egg, or someone else's

fresh ones? Was it fertility drugs, fertility treatments, or a night of wine with a young guy and his eager drone sperm? It's no one's business. The only thing that matters is that you did it. In the South, women your age are grannies.

YOU MAY BE THE OLDEST GRANDMOTHER SINCE GENESIS.

What if your daughter is like you, and waits until she's nearly fifty? You'll be a ninety-year-old first-time grandma. That is some Old Testament shit right there. On the bright side, it will be convenient. As your daughter goes into labor in the maternity ward, you will be close by, staring at the wall in the dementia ward.

OLD SH*TTY MOMS ARE GREAT SH*TTY MOMS.

You won't resent your kid for stealing your youth, because you squandered it all by yourself. Unlike the young moms, you can't blame any career setbacks on mommy-tracking. Your accomplishments are your pride, and the lack of them is your fault. But don't be hard on yourself—if you couldn't get it together before you had the baby, you probably weren't ever gonna get it together.

YOU HAVE PERSPECTIVE.

You can appreciate little moments because you have proof that life goes by quickly: your own middle age. Does a twenty-year-old mom understand that life is short? Nope. To her, life is taking forever. (Mostly because she can't drink yet.)

MAKE THINGS EASY.

Move to a coast. If you're the only old mom at the park, you can't possibly be living in New York or California. Move. Be among your people, old mom. There is strength in numbers, and other old moms need you to confirm the outside temperature, in case they have a hot flash.

 Remember: Instead of contributing to a college fund, get a good life insurance policy. You will probably die before your kid's student loans kick in.

CHAPTER 26

Young Moms:
Way to Ruin Your Life Early!

Well, well, well. Somebody didn't get the memo called "You Can Have a Life First." While other women your age were celebrating their quinceañeras, studying for the SATs, or graduating from college, you had a baby. You did not fall for that Gen-X hype about having it all. Unlike your old mom counterpart, you decided to do the hard stuff first.

It matters not how you got to motherhood—clumsy prom love or just family tradition. The point is, when your kids are out of the house, you'll be in your forties. Maybe even late thirties.

God damn you.

You and your still-flat abs. You and your easy delivery. You and your eyes without dark circles, no matter how many times your baby wakes you up. Don't you dare turn the page! You're gonna sit here and read this entire chapter. Take it like a man, you little girl.

Young Sh*tty Mom, you will find no empathy here, precisely because you are young. This is how good you have it: If you were a stripper, after the baby came, you could be back on the pole in two weeks like nothing happened. You'll even get extra tips from guys with a breastfeeding fetish.

Unfair.

The following tips will help you live among old and regular-age moms, who will understandably want to scratch your eyes out.

* **Watch your mouth.** Never say, "Oh, I never wanted to be one of those 'old moms.' " You may be speaking to "one of

those old moms" who's had so much Botox that she looks your age. Anyone who defies nature by giving birth in her forties is not likely to allow wrinkles to ruin her forehead.

* **Show some respect.** Old moms are Juvéderm pioneers whose brave work in the elimination of marionette lines will make your old age less wrinkled. By the time you get old, they may have figured out how to fix necks.

* **Pretend you understand their references.** If they start talking about the Pretenders or the Beastie Boys or the Cure or Boyz II Men, just nod and smile. You can Google their dinosaur bands later, when they're not looking.

   (Actually, if you have a smartphone, you can Google even when they are looking, because chances are, they can't see. And they're too vain to pull out reading glasses.)

* **Don't ruin it!** Use birth control until the doctor has confirmed that you are in full-blown menopause. You don't want to be a young mom and an old mom. That would mean your entire life is all mom. That only works if your last name is Duggar and TLC is offering you a show.

 Remember: You missed out on some wild times (not including the one that got you pregnant at sixteen). Your forties will be everyone else's twenties.

CHAPTER 27

Your "Friend" Hired a Bilingual Nanny

Like all mothers, you want to give your child every advantage. You want your kid to win. You want your kid to crawl to the top of life's scrap heap and rule the junkyard until they're stabbed in the back by a younger, more ambitious version of themselves.

It's the American dream.

You do as much as you can afford. The best private school, or the shittiest apartment in the best school district. Music lessons, sports, quality time, reading from books not screens, a rarely used IKEA easel in the family room. In kindergarten, it's your four-year-old vs. your friend's five-year-old (your friend red-shirted), and the winner of that round advances to the finals against the smartest kids from Asia and India.

Just when you think you've covered every base, and your kid has a chance of succeeding in this awful global economy, you are introduced to Jiao, your friend's Chinese nanny.

Second language. Forgot that! Damn it. No one in your family speaks anything but English.

Of course, it wasn't always that way. Fifty or two hundred years ago, your smelly, hungry ancestors came to America fluent in Italian, Russian, Swahili, or Japanese. They settled in some wretched ethnic enclave or homesteaded on a rocky dustbowl acre only to have their lazy descendants fully assimilate with the WASP neighbors and, in the process, lose the native language.

Now that language is necessary. It's great for the kid's brain and future job prospects. Take a moment here to curse your dumb family for allowing the language to die. *Meshugenah. Puta. Merde.*

Now what? You may be tempted to give up. Quit the piano lessons and gymnastics classes, sell the easel on Craigslist, and just let your kids watch cartoons ten hours a day.

Don't panic, mama. Not yet.

FLUENCY IN CHINESE IS NOT A PREDICTOR OF SUCCESS.

Look at the 2012 race for the Republican presidential nomination. Jon Huntsman spoke Mandarin and he never polled above 1 percent. He was creamed by Mitt Romney, who speaks French—the tongue of a fallen empire and Canada's least loyal province, Quebec. And of course, George W. Bush barely speaks English at all and he was president for eight years.

Your kid still has a shot.

GET YOUR KID INTO A PUBLIC DUAL-LANGUAGE IMMERSION SCHOOL.

Any second language will do. (Except Armenian. C'mon—get serious.) The fact that your kid is learning one at all is what's important.

SOME SECOND LANGUAGES ARE CHEAPER THAN OTHERS.

There's probably no polite way to say that Mexican nannies are about ten times more affordable than Asian ones. It's not right, it just is. Don't be a snob, Spanish is easy. *Es muy fácil!* Spanish uses the same alphabet as English, which means you can help with the homework. And Univision is the only TV network that is truly committed to its soap operas. What the hell are you waiting for?

IT'S IMPOSSIBLE TO MONITOR A NANNY YOU DON'T UNDERSTAND.

Don't assume your friend's nanny spends all day reading *The Art of War* in its original Chinese to her charge. If the nanny is teaching the kid any Chinese at all, it's probably phrases like "Your parents owe me $2,000 in overtime" and "Your mom keeps a filthy house." All other times, she's texting her boyfriend, just like a Colombian nanny.

SPEAKING A SECOND LANGUAGE ALL DAY LONG MAKES A PERSON HUNGRY.

If your kid ends up being one of the unwashed English-onlies, don't fret. As the federal government tightens the noose on illegal immigrants, more and more low-paying jobs will go to unskilled *Americans*. English-speaking-only Americans. In other words, your kid will always have work. Those foot-long sandwiches at Subway don't make themselves!

 Remember: There's always high school. While your kid won't become fluent by taking high school Spanish 1–5, she will be able to ask for directions in downtown Los Angeles. And maybe that's enough.

CHAPTER 28

How to Deal with Moms Who Exercise

Sometimes you're in survival mode. Life has dealt you a blow. You're trying to get back on your feet or even just your knees. During these times, it's OK to limit your friendships to other bare-minimum moms. Women who aren't going to throw their mom-compliments in your face.

Or their abs.

Moms who exercise regularly and look great can be a danger to your mental health. They walk up and down their driveway, with an inch of six-pack visible in the space where the Lululemon tank top and the Lululemon pants should touch.

One day, to be polite, you may decide to ask one of these moms what her secret is. Huge mistake! Get back in the house. Say anything: Fake that you just got your period! You're in a bad headspace. The last thing you need to know is:

"I run six miles every morning before work!"

Oh my God. You live next door to someone disciplined and dedicated. Some people would consider that reason enough to move.

"Oh, I wish I could do that," you say, "but I can't because I have to be at work so early."

OK, nice save. And it's true. You have to be to work at eight A.M., and drop the kids off to school, which means you are in the car at 7:30. There's no way you could run, shower, and get the kids dressed and fed by 7:30 A.M.

Phew.

If she was a decent person, she would let you enjoy your excuse, which is as rock-solid as her triceps.

Oh, no.

"Me too! I have to be at my desk at eight A.M.!"

Punch in the gut. Low blow. OK, time to let her have it. Load your Excuse Gun with a round of My Husband Left Me Bullets and aim it at her head.

"Well," you say, "I'm a single mom, and I have to get the kids ready for school all by myse—"

"Me too! That's why I'm on the treadmill at five A.M., before the kids even wake up!"

Abort, abort! You're wounded! Your gun misfired! You've been hit by the local "Me Too Mom." She has the same challenges as you ("Me too!"), yet manages to make time to exercise. And read a novel. And cook dinner. And date. And everything else you wish you could do but can't. At least not right now.

Surrender. Put your weapon down and crawl away. Life is cyclical and you're in a down cycle. Or, to put it another way, sometimes you're Germany before World War II, and sometimes you're Germany after it. Like Germany, you'll be back.

 Remember: One day you'll be the hot Me Too Mom that your depressed neighbors avoid.

The "'Me Too, And' Mom"

Even more demoralizing than the "Me Too Mom" is the " 'Me Too, And' Mom." While the "Me Too Mom" is just a better version of you, the " 'Me Too, And' Mom" lives your life . . . with an added degree of difficulty that makes everything harder. And she does it with a better attitude. She's a saint. You're a shit.

Examples of her chirpy responses to your woes:

"You're divorced? Me too, and I get no child support!"

"Your kid is on the spectrum? So are my triplets—both sets!"

"You're married, and a paraplegic? I'm a single quad!"

CHAPTER 29

Single Moms:
Sorry, but No One Will Trust You
Until You Get Married

"It is a truth universally acknowledged that a single mother in possession of her children must be in want of a nap."
—*Pride & Prejudice 2*, in which Mr. Darcy leaves
Elizabeth Bennet and their two children for Caroline Bingley

Every single-mom book can be boiled down to these eight learned lessons:

1. Being a single mom is hard, but not as hard as living with an asshole.
2. Beware your next crush. Your taste in men is suspect.
3. In 1970s and '80s TV icons terms, raising a kid on your own is 1 percent Murphy Brown and 99 percent Alice.
4. Most married women unconsciously believe that you will infect them with divorce cooties.
5. Learn to make basic repairs, or join Angie's List and hire someone with four stars to do it for you.
6. During election cycles, politicians will use you to rattle their base. The Republicans will shit on you and the Democrats will lionize you. After it's all over, nothing will change.
7. Cheer up. Lots of successful people were raised by single moms:
   ∗ President Barack Obama (the first African-American president)

* Michael Phelps (eight gold medals in a single Olympics)
* Louis C.K. (amazingly prolific comedian)
* Ted Bundy (amazingly prolific serial killer)

8. One day, out of nowhere, a married mom will say something along the lines of "Jim is gone so much because of work, I feel like a single mom!"

That statement is the mom equivalent of the assassination of Archduke Ferdinand. The awful silence that follows could easily escalate into the war to end all wars. Advice to both parties:

Single Mom: Remember, it is illegal to put your hands around someone's throat, no matter how ridiculous their comments.

Married Mom: Shut it. Shut your mouth. Shut your mouth before you are strangled to death.

Here's the difference between a single mom and a married mom whose husband travels three weeks out of the month. The husband eventually comes back. The single mom, depending on her ex's participation, never, rarely, or infrequently gets a day off. It's the court case of *Fucking Exhausted v. Totally Fucking Exhausted.*

Remember: Beware the man who's too eager to become a stepfather. The good ones realize what a huge commitment it is. Anyone who isn't scared shitless is a creep.

NOMS (NON-MOMS)

CHAPTER 30

The Nom at Work Who Thinks Her Dog Is a Child

At times, modern language is insufficient. Humans have been speaking for tens of thousands of years, yet we are unable to convey adequate sympathy when in the face of tragedy. We often say, "There are no words." Less traumatic situations also highlight our lingual impotence, like when that woman at work says, "Wanna see a picture of my kid?" and then pulls out a photograph of a dog.

It is no use in pointing out the obvious flaws in her analogy. (If you want to go out of town for a weekend, you can't leave your kid in the backyard and ask your neighbors to give him food and water. When your kid destroys your furniture, you can't drop him off at the pound. Et cetera.)

The tricky thing here is that she actually does love her dog more than you love your child. The proof is in the cubicles. How many pictures of your kid have you tacked to your dividers? One, two, three... four. Really? And you call yourself a mother?

Now, let's drop by her work space. Multiple corkboard partitions hold twenty or so photos of a golden Lab mix named Raffles, each printed on specialty photo-stock paper. Raffles at a Halloween party, dressed as a cat. Raffles ringing in the New Year, wearing a pair of oversized "2007" glasses. Raffles watching *Animal Planet*.

Her desk is a cemetery of framed photos of Raffles's deceased predecessor, another golden Lab mix named Pickles. Although Raffles and Pickles are identical to the naked eye, do not confuse them.

Because they are so different.

For example, Pickles—Do you have a moment? Your meeting isn't for five minutes, right? Great. Pull up a chair. Pickles—she's in the green collar—used to looooove to chase squirrels up trees. She'd sit there at the base of the trunk and bark. Sometimes she'd try to climb the tree—never caught one, but loved trying. But Raffles—complete opposite. Doesn't even *notice* squirrels. In fact . . . See that picture of Raffles in the park? See that tail peeking out from behind the bush? That's right, it's a squirrel! And Raffles doesn't even care! Look at her face, she's like, "I don't care!"

There are no words.

Moms can't win this unannounced competition. You'll never know as much about your kid as she knows about her dog, especially after your kid gets his driver's license.

 Remember: "Dog" spelled backward is "God." And "kid" spelled backward is "dik."

Things That Other People Love More Than You Love Your Kid

Dog lovers aren't the only people who can out-love a Sh*tty Mom.

A Belieber and Justin Bieber.

Justin Bieber fans feel a love so deep and true that you should tremble in its presence. Perhaps you claim that you would die to save your child's life. Big deal. A Belieber would die to meet Justin Bieber. Just to *meet* him. You meet your child every day and you aren't dead. That's because you don't understand love.

Your first boyfriend (who, in retrospect, was totally gay) and your black rubber Madonna bracelets.

Have you ever caressed your baby's face with the same gentle awe that Ethan (who, oddly enough, never pressured you to have sex) once caressed your collection of one hundred Madonna bracelets?

Your second boyfriend (six years older than you) and his Chevy IROC.

Has your child ever been washed as thoroughly as Kenny washed his Camaro every Saturday morning? Let Sh*tty Mom answer this: No.

That never-married forty-five-year-old guy who lives down the street and his *Star Wars* figurines.

You've only talked to that guy once, but it's obvious that his special-edition Boba Fett action figure is a greater source of pride to him than your son is to you. It makes sense: Your kid is just another one of the seven billion people on this planet. That particular Boba Fett is a collector's item.

CHAPTER 31

How to Stay Friends with a Nom You Used to Party With

Remember that mom-friend you had in your twenties? The frazzled, distracted friend who would talk and parent at the same time? You'd call to chat about your boyfriend and she'd say, "Gosh, I'm so sorry—ASHLEY, PUT THAT DOWN RIGHT NOW! DON'T MAKE ME COME OVER THERE. Sorry, yeah, so—ASHLEY, DO YOU WANT A TIME OUT?"

That's you now.

Babies take up space. Every child you have will knock about six people out of your life. You can't pick which ones either. A good friend will fall away and you won't notice until you realize you weren't invited to her wedding.

You're a Pilgrim. You left the Old World to start a new life in America. Stop looking back, wondering how your single friends in Merry Olde England are doing. They are having a great time, contracting syphilis from royal princes. Stop trying to organize a girls' night out. Leave these ladies alone. They don't know you anymore. You've adopted the ways of the natives. What's this "maize" you're eating?

Of course there are friendships you don't want to lose. You have a few options:

SOCIAL NETWORKING.

Facebook allows you to be involved in someone's life, without speaking to them or even putting on a bra. It's like working on your friendships, from home. Telefriending. When an old friend posts a status update, "like" it. That's it. Doesn't matter what the status is. "Tired of *Dancing with the Stars*." LIKE. "Ate pancakes, gonna throw up." LIKE. "I'll say one thing about Hitler, he knew how to build a highway." LIKE.

Your "like" lets them know you were thinking about them—at least for four seconds. You may not have time for a call, or coffee, or a night out, but you can always find time for a "like."

WAIT THEM OUT.

The Pilgrims never looked back, but they did welcome other immigrants who sailed to their shores. Many of your childless friends will one day land on your doorstep—with an infant in tow.

Remember: If your friends gave a damn about you, they'd get pregnant, too.

Yes, You Were Once That Annoying

One day you'll notice that all of the stupid things that you, in your Nom state, once said to moms are being said to you:

Nom: "Is she two now?"
You: "No, she's four."
Nom: "Oh! I am soooo not a 'kid person,' I can't even tell a baby from a kindergartner!"

Oh, ha ha ha. Aren't you the lucky one, so oblivious, so not a "kid person." Sh*tty Mom has the feeling that one day, you will know exactly the difference between a two-year-old and a four-year-old. Just you wait.

. . . .

Nom: "If I ever did have kids I would [x]." With x equaling "a child-rearing idea that sounds great, but in real life is impractical or insane." Examples of x:

* "only speak to them in French"
* "get rid of the TV"
* "use cloth diapers"
* "breastfeed until the baby weans itself"
* "quit my job and stay at home"
* "keep going until I have a girl"

. . . .

Nom: "I don't want kids."

Ah yes, that old chestnut. Usually said with certainty, approximately two years before conceiving. Warn your Nom friend that not wanting kids will not prevent her from having them.

CHAPTER 32

"Oh, C'mon, Just Bring Your Kid, It Will Be Fun!"

Remember when your mom told you to use her as an excuse for not succumbing to peer pressure? "Honey, if you want to get out of smoking pot, you just tell your friends that your mom is very violent and will beat you if you get high."

Whether or not you actually used her line to, uh, "get out of" smoking pot (she was so naive), the point is, your mom was willing to be the fall guy. Now it's your baby's turn. Instead of telling your friends, "I can't . . . my mom won't let me," you'll tell them, "I can't . . . the baby . . ."

And you won't even have to finish the sentence. It's understood. The baby. The goddamn baby.

Your baby is many things: a joy, a miracle, a nonstop piss and loose stool factory. She is also a GET OUT OF THE NICKELBACK CONCERT FREE card. The greatest excuse since dogs began eating homework. All those stupid things you did because you suck at saying no? Those days are over. Your baby will give you the backbone you've always longed for, and she'll do it by sucking the life out of you.

Having a baby is the female version of a rich man losing his inheritance. Now you find out who your real friends are.

It takes awhile to weed out the weak ones. They can't comprehend how different your life is now. One invites you to see her boyfriend's band. Another invites you to an art gallery. They will attribute your first two "no"s to temporary insanity brought on by childbirth. They'll get suspicious around the third "no," and by the fourth, they are gone. In their eyes, you have abandoned them. You don't even care that Jen is banging a drummer because you're so obsessed with your damn baby.

Well, good riddance. Don't let the door hit you on the way out, you happy, well-rested, slim-waisted Nom. And don't come back, until you're sallow-skinned and seven months along.

Except . . . there's always that one friend who refuses to go away. It's the friend who says, "Just bring the baby. It'll be fun!"

Her innocence is infuriating. It reminds you of the growing distance between you and your old life. Your friend thinks it would be "fun" to bring the baby to a wine bar that has free jazz on Sunday afternoons, while you know it will be hell. Carrots, sippy cups, diapers, wipes, and a change of clothes.

At a wine bar. Fun. Ha.

End it once and for all by taking your friend up on her offer. Say "yes." Bring your two-year-old daughter and make sure she didn't nap. Unleash the dogs of hell that is a toddler meltdown. Let your child's cries etch new neural pathways to the pain center in your friend's brain. Let your friend see your life now. Loud. Exhausting. Embarrassing. Endless.

She will never suggest it again.

 Remember: It's OK to say, "What part of 'No, I have a kid, call me in eighteen years' don't you understand?"

Guide for Noms Who Just Won't Go Away

So you're the Nom we've been talking about. The Nom who can't take a hint. The Nom who won't let her best friend completely abandon her for Baby Island. Even though that pal of yours took Sh*tty Mom's advice and let her two-year-old ruin your fancy, single-people wine tasting.

Your tenacity is admirable. You have a good heart, and quite frankly, she doesn't deserve you. And she isn't done trying to crush your spirit. All you can do is be prepared to entertain her baby the next time you insist she bring him out to lunch. Try to fit at least one of these things in your stylish, small clutch:

* **A box of crayons.** Kids are always ready to draw. And one day, just because, sign your credit card slip with Burnt Sienna.
* **Coins.** They're fun to stack, fun to count. Also fun to swallow, so they aren't good for a small baby.
* **Wipes.** Kids like to wipe things (except their nose when it's runny). Bring a small container of wipes and your table will gleam.
* **Keys and a smartphone.** If you forgot everything listed above but you still have keys and a smartphone, you are set. The baby will love the keys and his mother will love the smartphone.

YOU AREN'T PARANOID, EVERYONE DOES HATE YOUR BABY

CHAPTER 33

Tantrum at a Tar/Wal/K/Sam's/Mart/Club/Get (or Sears)!

Kids let you know it's coming. Their eyes grow dead and dull, like a killer's. Their limbs jerk, and their sticky hands begin frantically searching for hair to pull. They start shouting, "No!" and "I can do it by MYSELF." You have only seconds to decide: Do you finish up what you're doing, or leave?

It depends where you are. Should other people be subjected to your kid's tantrum? Not at a movie, restaurant, or church. Basically, any place with a cover charge. (And tithing is a cover charge—to God.) Don't be a dick and ruin someone else's good time. Yes, it sucks, but it's temporary. Before you know it, your awful toddler will morph into a sullen teenager that will refuse to be seen with you.

Then you're home free.

However, if you're at the mall or any store that sells kids' stuff, it's your call. Absolve yourself of guilt. Stores are trying to attract your child's attention. They want her to terrorize you until you are too tired to fight back. They arrange their shelves so that she will repeat "I want" a hundred times in a row until you sigh "All right" and buy her the doll, the action figure, or the Snickers bar.

Stores get what they deserve.

Target and Walmart ought to have alarms that moms can sound when they spot a warning sign. Ideally, a winged Target Team Member would fly you, your child, and your full cart to the parking lot. As you buckle in your kid, the Target Team Member would ring up your purchases, then put them in the car. And, while we're fantasizing, it would be nice if all tantrums occurred at a Victoria's Secret. To let their customers know that lingerie has consequences.

You may feel you ought to leave before your business is taken care of.

"Everyone's looking at me and thinking I'm a terrible mother," you fear. Well, you are right. They are. But what those people don't know is that you are providing a service. Your child is a PSA on parenthood. Because of you, condom sales are skyrocketing. The mall's office supply store is experiencing a run on Sharpie pens, bought by young women who will use them to write "Take BC pill!" on the back of their hands. All so they don't become you: a trapped, helpless thing at the mall. Your child is contributing to the local economy. Pat her on the back—once she stops arching it. If people won't think you're a terrible mom, they will think that motherhood is a terrible thing.

If you refuse to cave in, look in your purse. Do you have food? No? Can you take some off a store shelf and pay for it when you get to the cash register? Do that. Then buy a Sharpie pen from the office supply store and write "Bring food!" on the back of your hand.

 Remember: Spanking, while cathartic, merely increases the noise, and you can't beat your kids for being tired or hungry. Save the physical abuse for something special, like when they crash your car or get into your liquor.

When Your Child Observes That the Woman Standing in Your Checkout Line Appears to Have Stopped Dieting in 2004

If your kid isn't tantruming in the store, he's embarrassing you by pointing to larger shoppers and saying, "Mommy, that lady is fat!" It's important to note that your son is not trying to be a jerk—he's just shouting what you and all the other grown-ups are silently thinking. Kids are nature's profilers.

What can you do?

You can't tell your kid not to notice if someone is big, tall, short, bald, hairy, white, or black. They will grow up to be terrible police officers, ineffective fiction writers, and horrible at telling jokes about three different types of people who simultaneously walk into a bar. But kids do need to know that it is rude to call a person fat to their face. For God's sake, make sure they're out of earshot.

Part of socializing in a Western culture means lying, constantly. Not only do you not tell a woman she is fat, you ask her if she has lost weight. Especially if it's clear she has not. Does your friend, who just got divorced, look awful? Insist she's never looked better and demand to know her secret. Some thoughts must stay in one's head, caged like animals, until they can be let out. This is how deals are made, legislation is passed, and treaties are signed. Wait until the old man excuses himself before you talk about his hunchback. Wait until the president of Iran leaves the U.N. before you say, "If that guy thinks we're gonna let him build a nuclear bomb, he's crazy."

CHAPTER 34

Stop Looking for a Great Babysitter and Settle for One Who Shows Up On Time

If you are in the market for a babysitter, you either just had your first baby, or your old sitter quit. You gotta break someone in, fast.

* **Do not trust your friends.** No one gives up a good sitter. If a "friend" recommends hers, rest assured it is her "C" sitter. Her backup's backup. It's the sitter that eats food labeled "do not eat" and turns the channel even though the DVR is recording, so that three minutes into the season finale of *Breaking Bad*, you will be watching *Teen Mom*. You are getting someone else's sloppy seconds. Meanwhile, her "A" sitter, the one who shows up on time and never minds if you're home late... that sitter is a secret, like a teen pregnancy in the '50s.

   You are on your own. You are Scarlett O'Hara after Rhett dumped her on the way to Tara. Helpless Melanie is nursing in your wagon, and your reins are steering a dying nag through Yankee-held territory.

* **Scope out your neighborhood.** Is there a clever-eyed thirteen-year-old, or an empty-nested fifty-year-old? Pick wisely, because this person will spend hours in your house, unsupervised. She may find your tax records or stumble upon your vibrator(s). She could take pictures of the scis-

sors on the changing table and tweet them to CPS. You leave yourself open to ruin.

* **Post an ad on Craigslist.** Before you open the first response, decide how important it is that the sitter know the difference between "their" and "they're."

* **Gender profile.** Illegal? Yes. But this is not a federal job, it's babysitting. No one will know. And while no one's saying that a man should not be allowed to babysit, Sh*tty Mom is saying that men on Craigslist should not be allowed to babysit. What if he clicked on "childcare" only because he got no response from "men seeking women"?

* **Lower your standards.** It would be great if sitters got down on their knees and engaged their charges. But seeing as how your kid bores you, it's a stretch to think the sitter will enjoy sitting on your floor, playing LEGOs. In fact, if she's anything like the great 1970s babysitters of our youth, she will play with your kid until you've backed the car out of the driveway. Then she'll drop the toys and let your kid watch TV while she talks to her boyfriend for three hours.

Just as the good Lord intended.

 Remember: Oh, to be a babysitter, and live in a world where "Do Not Eat" means "Please Eat," and "Be here at eight" means "Text me at 8:10 to say you're running late."

CHAPTER 35

Yes, the Babysitter Is Judging You

It was just yesterday that you were fourteen years old, out with your friends on a Saturday night. Looking at magazines, listening to music, making out or getting felt up. Curfew was approaching, and you'd call your mom, begging her to let you out past ten . . . just this once. She'd say no and you'd close up shop. Pull David's hand out of your bra, button up your blouse. You'd get home five minutes late, and your mom would be sitting on the couch, waiting for you. Pissed. You'd stomp off to your room and plot life after your eighteenth birthday. You're gonna stay out all night. Every night. For the rest of your life.

Hell, yeah.

A few decades have gone by. You're a mom now. A woman. You've had jobs, paid rent, made a baby. For that alone, you deserve some goddamn respect. And now you're out on a Saturday night. Date night. You're wearing heels that hurt and the bottom half of your legs are shaved. Dinner was great. The wine is working, your man looks hot, and this place has a band. It's close to ten P.M. You ain't done yet.

Oh yes you are.

Your teenage babysitter just replied to your text. No, you may not stay out past ten. She has a track meet tomorrow morning. She's seeded first in two events, and she *told* you that when she took the job.

"pls b home at 10 like u sed"

You get back at 10:15. She and her mother, who's picking her up, are waiting on your couch. Waiting for your buzzed self. You apologize profusely and pay her till eleven, but it's not enough to wipe the pissed look out of their eyes. You're a jerk who doesn't put her kids to bed and comes home drunk.

And late.

Like prostitutes, babysitters are paid cash to do things that you do for free. And they don't even have to pay out to a pimp. They hold all the cards. All you can do is minimize their judgment and the guilt you might feel for going out.

* **You are allowed to leave your babies.** Movies must be seen, karaoke must be sung, and dinners must be had with the husband or that tall guy from Match.

* **Use more than one babysitter.** And make sure they don't know each other. Select from a different age bracket, class, race, religion, and ethnicity. Rotate them. If you're going out four nights in a row, bring in at least two babysitters.

  Multiple babysitters are good for the kids' emotional IQ. They'll learn how to talk all kinds of women into letting them stay up past nine. Kitchen cabinet politics—it's how presidents are made. The child who is adept at persuading an Asian teenager, a white grandma, and a middle-aged African-American into letting her blow through bedtime will grow up into the adult who rules the world.

 Remember: Whatever you do that requires a babysitter is no one's business.

CHAPTER 36

Motherfucking Babies on the Motherfucking Plane

You are trapped in an awful place (a plane) with awful people (passengers) who will hate you even though it's not your fault they can't afford to charter a private, child-free jet.

1. Babies are supposed to cry on planes.
Their eardrums are popping and they don't have the manual dexterity to perform the "hold your nose" trick. Crying is an appropriate response to pain, at any age. In fact, the babies who *should* be demonized on a plane are the ones who don't cry. What kind of baby sleeps through inner-ear pain? A terrifying baby! A dangerous baby! A baby with ice in its veins and a heart made of rocks. Yes, you may be suffering now, but remember: A baby who cries on a plane will not grow up to suffocate you in your sleep.

2. Make an effort to soothe your baby.
Feed, bounce, sing, and read. Check the diaper. You know the routine. The odds are that none of it will work, but your diligence makes you look good, and the real problem here isn't your crying baby....

3. The real problem: other passengers.
Aside from a few understanding grannies, you will be reviled from the moment you pre-board the plane. Hip-

sters will roll their eyes, and businessmen will start pounding gin and tonics like they've been cast in *Mad Men*.

4. Buck up.

One day, all of these douchebags will retire. They'll crack open their IRAs and realize they didn't save enough, having spent too much on things like airfare and plane booze. And what will they be forced to live on? Social Security. Which will be funded by taxes taken from the paycheck of your crying baby. Instead of shrinking in your seat, see your fellow passengers for who they really are: deadbeats who will spend their final years sucking on your baby's teat.

5. Tune out.

Put on your noise-canceling headphones, open a tab on your Amex, and crank up whatever music makes you feel young again.

6. But what about . . . Benadryl?

Yes, Benadryl will put your baby to sleep, but where's the fun in that? Can't every problem in life be temporarily solved with a few drops of Benadryl? Why not call this book *Booze and Benadryl*, and be done with it? C'mon, let's think outside the medicine box.

OH, I DON'T NEED THIS CHAPTER BECAUSE I HAVE AN IPAD.

Good for you. All your problems are solved. But guess what, sister? Batteries die, and planes get stuck on runways. For hours. And iPads don't pack themselves. By all means, bring it, but like all sure things in life, count on it to fall apart when you need it most.

Remember: These asshole passengers were themselves once asshole babies who ruined flights. And not the shitty flights of today, but wonderful flights with dressed-up stewardesses, free emergency-row seating, and a smoking section. They have some nerve criticizing you.

Ways to Make Your Kid Stop Kicking the Seat

Once, we sat in front of a mom who did not stop her child from kicking our seat, and the back pain lasted for days. Be a Sh*tty Mom, not an Extra Sh*tty Mom.

* Take your child on walks up and down the aisle. He will burn energy, and you can confront your accusers, eye to eye.
* Take off his shoes. If he does kick, it hurts his toes more. (And the person in front of you will hurt less.)
* Sit on his feet. If you are heavy—even better. Make that baby weight work for you.

CHAPTER 37

Miss Work Without Saying It's Because of Your Sick Kid

Your kid is sick, too sick to fool a teacher. He has to stay home. And you don't live in Sweden or Denmark, where they're cool with that. You live in America, where your employer can easily replace you with someone who has no kids. Or someone who has kids who don't get the flu. Or someone who has kids with the flu and has no problem sending them to school.

You have two options, depending on your marital or co-parenting situation.

1. Make his dad do it.

The odds are pretty high that staying home to care for a sick kid will hurt his career less than it will hurt yours. Sadly, the women at work love it when men are good fathers:

Female coworker (Donna): "Oh, isn't he wonderful! Stepping up and taking care of his children."

Female coworker (Kate): "Those poor kids, saddled with a mother who doesn't care."

Donna: "What a shame. Maybe he'll leave her one day, for the children's sake."

Kate: "Well, if he does, he can bring that fine ass of his over to my house."

Donna: "I hear that."

Which is the exact opposite of what happens when you are a good mother:

Donna: "Oh, she claims her kid is sick. Please. Didn't her kid get sick last year?"

Kate: "Yes. I wonder if she's making him sick. Do you think she has Munchausen syndrome?"

Donna: "I don't know, but if that kid of hers is gonna get the flu every winter, she should stay at home until he's in college."

Kate: "Exactly. And maybe she can get that fat ass of hers back in shape."

Donna: "I hear that."

2. You stay home, but tell no one why.

Actually, a good thing to do would be to travel back in time and tell no one that you even have a child. Especially if you are a single mom. No one wants to hear how hard it is, or how tired you are. That's *your* problem, honey. To married moms and the single Noms, you are their worst-case scenario. They look at you and say, "There but for the grace of God go I."

NO ONE IS YOUR ALLY.

* **Men without kids** don't want to be reminded that children exist. In fact, most of them don't want to be reminded that women can bear children. They are in the "whore" phase of their Madonna/Whore complex.

* **Men with kids** don't want to hear their own children whine for juice, much less yours.

* **Older women with kids** are annoyed that you're getting away with this. Back in the '90s, they got mommy-tracked if they stayed home with a sick child. You have it so goddamn easy.

* **Your excuse needs to be anything but the truth.** On the chart comparing the things that people secretly hate about women, staying home with a sick kid is one notch above being childless and happy. You will be penalized, even if it's in a subtle or small way. You must lie. And please, no fake deaths. This is not elementary school, and you're too old to have a dying grandmother.

  Jury duty. This is bulletproof, as long as your boss doesn't ask for paperwork.

  Anything financial: closing on a house, meeting with your accountant. An audit works particularly well here—most people believe that only winners or men attract the attention of the IRS.

  If you are under forty or pretending to be, consider acting as if you are hungover from a wild night. It makes you seem young and … not like someone's mother. Which we can agree is 100 percent less sexy than being a father.

If you're lucky:

* **Befriend a stay-at-home mom and see if you can do a trade-out.** Or pay her. Those ladies get no compensation and not enough respect.

* **A last-minute babysitting service.** They are expensive, but that frees you up to save the lies for when you *really* are hungover or being audited.

 Remember: No matter how supportive your coworkers pretend to be, it's a lie. And there's only one way to offset a lie, and that's to tell another lie.

How to Get a Job Working the Front Desk of a Top-notch Pediatrician

* Must be able to tell a parent to "have a seat," without making eye contact.

* Must be comfortable responding to every situation with the phrase "Have you signed in?" Examples:

"Excuse me, I have been waiting for over an hour."
"Have you signed in?"

"Excuse me, but it feels like my baby's temperature has gone up since we got here."
"Have you signed in?"

"Excuse me, but a man with a knife is standing behind you, and he says that he will stab you repeatedly if you ask me again if I have signed in."
"Have you signed in?"

* Must not express human emotion, unless the parent did not bring cash for the co-pay. And the only acceptable emotion is "annoyance."

* Must not tell a parent that the doctor is running late, especially if the parent asks, "Is the doctor running late?" Instead, double-check that the parent has signed in.

AWKWARD CONVERSATIONS

White Moms: How to Bounce Back After You Ask an African-American Mom if the Wrong African-American Child Is Hers

Note: While *Sh*tty Mom* is a book for mothers of every race, ethnicity, nationality, sexuality, and gender, the following chapter is written exclusively for white moms. Well-meaning white moms.

Let us first establish that you are a good person. You have only the best of intentions. You love that your white kids are friends with other-race kids. The black kid, the Hispanic kid, that Asian girl, that ethnically vague kid down the street with the brown curly hair (Arabian? Italian? Kardashian?). It's all good! You fully believe that diversity produces well-rounded children who will succeed in an America where, soon, whites will no longer be the majority.

Yay, you!

Here you are, at your daughter's Saturday morning gymnastics class, watching from the bleachers. In her class are two African-American girls, and in the bleachers with you are two African-American moms. One of the girls—the one with the cornrows—executes a nice, clean backbend. You are impressed. You want her mother to know that you are democratically excited about every child's accomplishment, even if they're black. (Don't worry, you didn't say that out loud.)

Unfortunately, you don't know which African-American woman is the mother of Backbend Girl. However, your keen eye observes that one of the moms has cornrows. Just like Backbend Girl! What are the odds that—STOP RIGHT NOW.

Please.

This is one of those things that, even if it goes well, will net you a nearly pointless victory. Who are you going to tell? Is there a whites-only message board where you can post about successfully matching the African-American mom to the African-American child?

And do you think the African-American mom gives a shit? Will she go onto her blacks-only message board and post that "white people are finally getting us"?

There's no winner in this scenario. There's only a loser who didn't lose as much as she could have.

Even worse: What if you guess wrong? What then? Will you panic and explain your cornrows theory? Will you realize how white you sound and overcorrect yourself by saying something worse? Or will you switch races completely and attempt to match the Chinese girl to the adoptive white mom? Only to find out that a) the Chinese girl is Japanese and b) she's not adopted. Good God, woman, you're spinning out of control!

A few things you can do:
* Say, "Oh, my mistake!"
* Stop talking.

Note to African-American moms: Please give Well-Meaning White Mom a break. She probably grew up in the last town in America to have no black people. She believes that your child's very existence will enrich her child's life. To her, you are the mystical mother of a fairy princess—with cornrows.)

 Remember: It's always OK to ask "Which kid is yours?"

CHAPTER 39

How to Get Rid of a Mom Who Wants to Stay Over During the Entire Playdate

The playdate is set. That mom you don't know very well, but whose daughter plays OK with yours, is dropping her child off at one P.M. That means from one till about... three-ish, your child will be occupied. And, in the world of parenting (and Orwell), Occupation = Freedom. Oh, you may have to referee a fight or two, pour some juice, pass out cookies... but that's a small price to pay for several ten-minute increments of solitude. You can Facebook, watch some *30 Rock*s, and finish reading last month's *Real Simple*.

Ahhh.

Mom and child arrive. You welcome them inside. Your kid drags hers to the bedroom. The mom follows. Yes, her child will be safe and happy here. You don't cook meth—in fact you barely cook food. The floor is clean-ish and the toys are mostly lead-free. The mom approves. You leave the children to play, and you move to escort the mom out the front door and she... sits down on your couch.

"So," she asks, picking up your *Real Simple*. "What do you do?"

It's over. Instead of enjoying some semi-alone time, you are stuck on a mom-date. Two hours of what the husbands do for a living, how well your kids sleep through the night: the vague chitchat that women engage in when the only thing they have in common is similar-age kids. If you absolutely can't fake it, you have two options:

1. **Include the mom in your plans.** Perhaps she thinks she *has* to stay over, and is as uncomfortable as you are. Pour alcohol. She's probably also behind on *30 Rock*. Best case: You make a friend. Worst case: The mom thinks you are a day drinker and never brings her kid over again. If she spreads the word, you will become popular with other day drinkers, and that can't be a bad thing.

2. **Just be honest, sort of.** Say, "You know, there's so much laundry and cleaning that I was hoping to get done while the girls played...." Then just trail off and stand there awkwardly. Chances are fifty-fifty that she will respond with "Me too! Do you mind if I come back at three?"
   And then you've made a real friend.

 Remember: If you want a new friend, open some wine. If you don't, open the door.

CHAPTER 40

"Your Daddy Is a Cheating Fuckbag" and Other Sentiments You Should Keep to Yourself

This is difficult, because it's something you have to *not* do. Every day. Forever.

So let's us grown-ups, pause to acknowledge that your ex is indeed a shithead. He is a Loretta Lynn song—he done you wrong. A no-good lyin' cheatin' drinkin' beatin' varmit rascal who made bad love and worse coffee. You are better off without him, and your kids don't have to see the two of you miserable together.

The divorce or breakup was a good thing.

Unfortunately, that fuckup is your kids' father, and no matter what he did to you (or them), they love him. It is one of the world's great injustices that you cannot speak the truth about that man without harming your kids.

Your best option is to say nothing negative in their presence. Which is easier written than done. Every day of your life will be a character test, and some days you will fail.

How can you refrain from saying shitty things about your ex in front of the kids?

1. **Say shitty things *to* your ex, via text.** There's no need to raise your voice on the phone or in person when you can type "YOU OWE ME CHILD SUPPORT" in exciting all caps.
2. **Say shitty things about him to your friends.** They never liked him anyway.

3. **Say shitty things about him on anonymous message boards.** Get instant feedback from other anonymous posters. Repeat until you are all bored.

4. **Tweet (but not under your name).** Create an anonymous Twitter account using a Gmail address and tweet his transgressions. And so that we can all follow along: hashtag #sh*ttymomsh*ttyex.

5. **Raise children who possess critical thinking skills.** One day they'll figure out that you did 90 percent of the work. And you will get your props during their valedictorian/ Heisman/inaugural speech.

6. **Have sex.** The importance of fresh genitals cannot be overstated. You don't have to marry this one either, OK? Get laid, then get out.

7. **Begin a new relationship.** Match.com is full of guys who hate their ex-wives as much as you hate your ex-husband. Meet! Mate! The friction caused by your vigorous hate-sex will create a new energy that can propel you both into healthier, happier relationships.

8. **If you were the asshole who ruined things, well, shut up—and hope the kids don't find out.**

 Remember: It's not your kid's fault that you're attracted to douchebags.

CHAPTER 41

When Strangers Assume
Your Long-Haired Boy Is a Girl

You and your two-year-old son are waiting in line at the grocery store. Your son has longish hair. He doesn't mind it and you can't bear to cut it. Especially now that his dad is going bald. Someone's got to have a mane in the family, right?

Prominently displayed in your cart is a box of Go Diego Go diapers. Your son is wearing a Thomas the Tank Engine T-shirt, and bending his hand into a finger gun, which he is aiming at human beings. All signs point to "boy." Nevertheless, the woman standing in line behind you says, "Oh my goodness, your daughter has such beautiful curls!"

You're cool. This happens sometimes. No biggie.

"Actually," you say, "he's my son, but thank you, I love his curls, too."

End of story, this chapter is over.

Actually, no. People hate making gaffes. It embarrasses them. Now this woman is embarrassed by her mistake. And if there's one thing embarrassed people need, it's someone to blame.

You.

"Well," says the woman, "if you don't want people to think he's a girl, then you should trim his hair!"

Oh, no. She went Boolean on your ass with an if/then statement. The "if/then," when applied to a parent and analyzed for subtext, is nearly always an insult. In this case, what she meant was, "*If* you were a better mother, *then* I wouldn't have thought your son was a girl."

What is to be done here? She is a stranger. This isn't a fight that will be fun to win, like the ones you have with your mother-in-law. If you are feeling feisty, you can toss back your own "*If* I was more of a bitch, *then* I'd say that the only thing that needs to be trimmed around here is your forty-five-inch waist."

But *if* you say that, *then* you are teaching your son to fight like a girl.

> **Remember:** The only babies that don't get mistaken for the wrong gender are baby girls whose ears have been pierced. And if you do that without being Hispanic, then you will be judged.

Five Things Your Four-Year-Old Son Will Learn if You Accidentally Bring Him into the Women's Locker Room at the YMCA, Instead of the Family Locker Room

* Naked ladies are mean and they yell when you look at them.

* Naked ladies should put more hair between their legs so they can look like Mommy.

* Naked ladies don't want to see my *Star Wars* backpack.

* Naked ladies don't care if I shot a thousand bad guys. Or a million bad guys. Or a million thousand bad guys.

* It's hard to walk with my eyes closed.

WE DIDN'T FORGET ABOUT YOU, SH*TTY DADS!

CHAPTER 42

He Wants Sex, You Want to Sew Your Legs Shut for Ten Years

First of all, you must have compassion for these men. After the baby is born, your man's body is exactly the same and yours is completely different. Your nipples are rough, and breathing causes your stomach to ripple like a jumped-on water bed. During the birth, your vagina was ripped apart or your body was cut open.

If you are a lesbian couple... one of you just experienced the miracle of childbirth and the other still looks hot. (And if you are two dads—well, carry on, you jerks.)

But these straight men, they are unchanged. And now that your pregnancy is over, they want things to go back to normal. They want fondling and touching and sex. They want you.

It would be sweet if it wasn't so incredibly painful.

What do you want? Sleep. Help. Your old body back. Just one day where you aren't worrying about SIDs or autism or BPA or preschool admission.

Neither of you will get your needs met, for a while. In the meantime:

ALLOW AND ENCOURAGE PORN.
Porn is an effective way for some men to relieve their genitals of excess sperm. (Surplus sperm, according to its many sufferers, is a medical condition more painful than losing a limb.)

You don't have to watch porn with your husband, but don't stand in his way. Unless you are going to let him watch it through your legs.

ON OCCASION, GIVE IT UP.

If you're not getting sleep, you probably feel and look like shit. But he doesn't care, and may not even notice. He just wants to have sex, and you're the one he's supposed to do it with. Guys are cute that way. Sex may make him more inclined to help you, which means you might get to sleep in on "your" morning to feed the baby. He's getting sex, you're getting sleep. Needs are being met. You will survive this.

RESTORATION OF THE CRUCIAL SEX:MASTURBATION RATIO.

Slowly, the "sex to masturbation ratio" will return to pre-baby levels. (S2M ratio being the amount of times you two have sex together vs. the amount of times he gives up and masturbates instead.) If, prior to the baby, you had sex two times for every five times he masturbated, then your S2M ratio was 2:5. For the first six weeks after the baby's arrival, it will be 0:40. Six months later, you will be at 1:20, and by the time your child is seven years old, you will be back to 2:5.

Or divorced.

 Remind yourself: You will get your desire back. Your top priority is to survive the first year without killing yourself, your baby, or his father.

CHAPTER 43

How to Make Your Husband or Babydaddy Stop Calling Your Son "Bro"

Had you known that the first words your husband would say to your newborn son would be "What's up, bro?" you probably wouldn't have mated with him. But it's too late now. However, you can and must nip Cool Dad in the bud. Address these points in your sit-down:

EXPLAIN THIS IS NOT ACCEPTABLE.

"Bro," like its 1990s predecessor "dude," is a peer-to-peer nickname *only*. Boys do not fear anyone who calls them "bro," and there comes a time in every boy's life when he needs to fear the wrath of his father. Because "Bro, I am so going to take away your driving privileges if you get a ticket" isn't going to make a sixteen-year-old follow the speed limit.

IT'S CONFUSING.

What if you have another male child? What then?

"Bro, please stop hitting your bro. Thanks, bros."

BRO'S FEMALE COMPLEMENT IS EVEN WORSE.

What if you have a daughter? And what if your daughter is walking in front of her brothers, but for safety's sake, you want the boys to walk ahead of her? Will Cool Dad stop your daughter and say, "Sweetheart, bros before hos"?

IT'S INACCURATE.

A father cannot also be his son's brother unless your family dynamics are incredibly dysfunctional. How can you demand your son get an A in science when his own father does not understand basic biology?

FACE IT, WE ARE WHAT WE ONCE DESPISED.

The very act of being a dad means that, for a decade, his kids will be embarrassed by the sight of him. No matter how rockin' he was as a single guy, he is a father now, and as such, everything he touches turns to lame. His retro T-shirts will be stupid, his tattoos will be tired, and his piercings will be weak. No dad is more embarrassing than the one trying to be cool.

Remember: Sons break away from their fathers, daughters laugh at their mothers.... We are doomed to become our parents and we can't "bro" our way out of it.

CHAPTER 44

*Sh*tty Mom* Ode
to the Stay-at-Home Dad

Stay-at-home dad
Your acronym is SAHD
Hard to believe that
You're a Princeton grad

On the first day, the baby
Reached for your nipple
On that first day
You poured yourself a triple

You'd really like to talk
To a grown-up
Damn! You gotta go,
The two-year-old has thrown up!

Mom makes the money
While you clean and cook
And read to your children
Goddamn book after book

In fact, if you read
One more rhyme by Dr. Seuss
You're gonna slip
Your head in a noose

It's lonely at the park
Cause you're the only guy
Moms shake their heads
And whisper "Why?"

Hey, that's your kid there!
That's why you stay awhile!
So back off bitches,
You're a SAHD, not a pedophile!

You play dolls with your daughters
And with your gay son
You pretend that tea parties
Are nothing but fun

Little do you know
That you've ruined them for life
Cause now they think guys
Are going to be nice

You get so much praise
For staying at home
Yet Sh*tty Moms get a book
And you get a "poem"

SAHD Recipe Book

The SAHD lifestyle does not come naturally to most American men. Mealtime can be particularly embarrassing. He can't cook, and he can't stand Rachael Ray's voice—there is truly no solution. And SAHD has many questions: Is peanut butter and jelly, on separate pieces of toast, a different meal than a peanut butter and jelly sandwich? If yes, then breakfast and lunch are taken care of, right? And the only meal to worry about is dinner. Right?

Oh, SAHD, you are so adorably male. How can you add some variety to your family's dinners without actually adding to your skill set? A few shitty tips:

* Try something French: Prepare eggs for scrambling, then flip them over into the "omelette" position. That's how French people do it.

* Try something Mexican: Melt cheese on a tortilla.

* Try something Greek: Start with a bowl of lettuce. Add olives, red onions, feta cheese, and olive oil.

* Try something Italian: Start with a bowl of pasta. Add olive oil, Parmesan cheese, lemon juice, and Italian parsley.

* Try something American: Order Chinese.

YES, IT'S OK TO HATE THE ZOO

CHAPTER 45

Animals That Need to Be Fired from Their Job at the Zoo

Sh*tty Mom gets that it's no easy task to run a zoo. There is the feeding and care of the animals in the zoo and then there is the feeding and care of the animals who live in the zoo. Wearing their tiny backpacks and complaining that everything is too far away. Looking like the stereotype of every American tourist in London.

However, after parking in a stadium lot, paying an admission charge of $15-plus per adult, and $12-plus per child, plus $9 for each small Pepsi, one's expectations escalate. A trip to the zoo can easily turn into a $100 day.

The point is: These animals are in show business and they need to be *on*. Not "circus animal" on, where they're dressed in outfits or sharing the stage with clowns. That's abuse. No, they only need to be "zoo animal" on. And all that means is awake. And visible.

Are you a zoo animal? Get out from behind the rock and move, goddamnit. C'mon, you're a jaguar. Act like it. You're gonna just sit there with your back to the crowd? You're so tired from your life of leisure that you can't roam and snarl a little? Lunge, or a formal complaint will be filed.

The problem with zoo animals is they have a job for life. There's no incentive to work hard—they're tenured. What zoo animals need is to have their livelihood be threatened by younger, sexier versions of themselves.

It appears that the reason zoos have so many animals is that on any given day, at least 50 percent of them call in sick. Or they hide. Or hibernate. The camouflagers are the worst. They force you to stare angrily into their bland habitat, convinced there's nothing there, until you notice out of the corner of your eye that one of the rocks just sneezed.

It's not as if they need to camouflage themselves. They're not being hunted. One can only conclude that the reason they're blending in with their surroundings at the zoo is that they're dicks.

It's clear that some animals need to be fired, while others should be given a raise and access to hotter trainers. An animal-by-animal breakdown:

ELEPHANTS They can't hide and they can't curl up in a hostile ball (hello, bears). Elephants stand in their fake savannas, flapping their ears and swinging food into their mouths with delightful trunks. If they are depressed to be out of Africa, they don't show it. Their attitude is excellent, and their resemblance to Dumbo, their representative in the cartoon world, makes them a favorite of the impossible-to-please toddler set.

Sh*tty Mom Recommendation: A 10 percent raise and double their office space.

BEARS Bears are awake for all of ten minutes a day. During those ten minutes, they hold a meeting and agree to pass out as soon as a parent says, "Oh look, Max, a bear!" Is there any act more cruel than falling asleep in full view of parents who have probably not slept in years? Just seeing them snore in the sun without flinching when children cry can inspire the most committed vegan to buy a hunting rifle. If bears were human, they would tap-dance in front of amputees.

Sh*tty Mom Recommendation: Two days in a game preserve with Sarah Palin.

ALLIGATORS Even when they're motionless, their teeth stick out of their mouths. They look exciting and murderous. Alligators (and crocodiles) are effortlessly terrifying.

Sh*tty Mom Recommendation: 15 percent raise, and feed them one loud teenager a day.

FLAMINGOS Is there anything more delightful than a flock of high-stepping pink flamingos? Walking deliberately on their stick legs, as if waiting for cocktails to be served?

Sh*tty Mom Recommendation: Give these birds the martini they were so obviously born to drink.

PARROTS Parrots can talk. It's unbelievable that other birds haven't noticed the success that parrots enjoy and asked themselves why. "Why do the kids get excited about that noisy blue and green thing, and not me, a bald fucking eagle?"

Well, bald eagle, instead of spending all day posing for country-music album covers, or whatever it is you do now that you're not nearly extinct, maybe you should look outside yourself and see that parrots speak English. And Spanish, and Russian, and every other language they've been exposed to. Like Ari Gold in *Entourage*, parrots know how to play the game. And bald eagle, they are rewarded for it.

(Moms, if you can't afford a bilingual nanny and are on the waiting list for a dual-language-immersion school, consider buying a Spanish-speaking parrot.)

Sh*tty Mom Recommendation: Move the parrots from the aviary to the reception area, where they can welcome visitors.

LEOPARDS For too long, leopards have coasted on their spots. Do leopards know that Robert Lopshire wrote a book called *Put Me in the Zoo*, and that the leopard in the book has spots that change colors? Kids run to the leopard area expecting an animal with red, blue, and yellow spots. Being beige and lying around on a flat rock, flexing a paw every now and then, ain't cutting it.

Sh*tty Mom Recommendation: Move them next to the monkeys.

MONKEYS Monkeys are triple threats: They fly, they swing, and they masturbate. While bears plot new ways to ignore you, monkeys discuss new ways to revolt you. They take classes like "Intro to Picking a Bug Off Another Monkey, Then Eating It" and "Advanced Semen Throwing." They hoot, make creepy eye contact, and lick their lips salaciously. Monkeys live the life that a sex offender can only dream of.

Sh*tty Mom Recommendation: Double their salary, give them porn, and let the monkey cage stay open until one A.M. on weekends.

GORILLAS Gorillas think they are too good for this gig, and they're right. Unlike monkeys, gorillas are smart. They are stronger than us and they can maneuver on all fours (at any time, not just on Saturday night). If gorillas and dolphins were to ever join forces, the human race would be eliminated. Don't count on a *Planet of the Apes*–like uprising, because real gorillas will not enslave us. They will kill us. Gorillas would love nothing more than to wrap their opposable thumbs around our weak necks and strangle us until we are dead.

By the way, gorillas read the study that claimed orangutans are the smartest apes, and the scientist who wrote it is number one on their to-die list. For our own safety, we should not allow gorillas to watch us. They are taking notes.

Sh*tty Mom Recommendation: Put them behind a one-way mirror.

FEMALE LIONS When kids think "lion," they think "mane." It's sexist and fur-ist, but in today's world, a bare-necked female lion is boring. It's extremely disappointing to send your children toward the lion's den, only to be told that the male lion is "taking the day off but it's OK, because his substitute, Sandy, a lioness, is more than capable of filling in!"

Oh really, zoo? Then please explain why this conversation is happening:

"Mama, where's the lion?"

"That's the lion, right there. Her name is Sandy."

"That's not a lion!"

"Yes it is. That's a mama lion."

"That's not a lion. You're lying to me."

"Honey, I'm not 'lion' to you."

"Why are you laughing, Mama? YOU'RE MAKING FUN OF ME I HATE YOU!"

Thanks for this $100 meltdown, zoo. Guess what? This argument can be had for free in the produce section of the grocery store:

"Mama, is that a orange?"

"No, it's a tangerine."

"No it's not, it's a orange."

"It looks like AN orange, but actually it's a different fruit called a tangerine. Now ... 'orange' you glad I explained that to you?"

"Why are you laughing, Mama? YOU'RE MAKING FUN OF ME I HATE YOU!"

Sh*tty Mom Recommendation: Hate to be sexist against our own, but female lions ought to accept the zoo's generous buyout offer and retire.

 Remember: You can't go wrong with animals that masturbate.

CHAPTER 46

Worst Children's Book: *The Giving Tree* vs. *Love You Forever*

Any mom who follows the parenting model of the protagonist in Shel Silverstein's *The Giving Tree* is creating a monster. An entitled asshole who will expect the women in his life to allow themselves to be dismembered in the pursuit of his temporary happiness.

Mothers of sons: Remember, you are raising our daughters' boyfriends and husbands. Please don't let our girls hook up with a jerk who thinks he's special because he does the dishes once a month. Put down *The Giving Tree* and pick up *Curious George*. If our daughters must get knocked up, let it be by a gentle animal lover who has a good job.

Mothers of daughters: Protest at any bookstore that sells this douchebag manifesto. Demand that it come with a warning label: "Reading this book may cause your son to expect someone else to fold his laundry for the rest of his single life."

As bad as *The Giving Tree* is, it's a thousand times better than Robert Munsch's *Love You Forever*, a most deceptive children's book. The cover looks harmless enough: a two-year-old, raising hell in the bathroom. It starts fine, with Mother singing a sweet lullaby to her baby about loving him forever. Yup, done that. Now we witness the passage of time. Two pages later, Mother crawls into her young son's bedroom and spies on him as he sleeps. Aside from the crawling, she is still in normal territory.

This continues as the boy turns nine. The reader is beginning to feel slightly uncomfortable. How long can Mother keep this up?

No need to wonder. Turn the page. Guess who just snuck into her teenage son's bedroom for a late-night cuddle? Quick, call the police! A horrible Oedipal relationship is in the making. Everyone knows that when teenage boys go to bed, they don't sleep. They masturbate. Relentlessly, all night long, until their fingers break off. Then they switch hands. Then they use their feet. Even zoo monkeys are appalled. Any mother who sneaks up on her teenage son when he thinks he is alone in the dark is going to be hit by cross fire.

(Tip: Stay out of your teenage son's room until he goes to college. Then enter it with a power washer and safety goggles.)

Oh, the story's not over. Instead of just embracing the empty nest, Mother takes to stalking her son and his new family. (The son's wife, meanwhile, is nowhere to be found. He probably stabbed her to death, as he screamed over and over again, "Leave me alone, Mother!") On the last page, Mother is presumed dead, and the son sings to his own baby.

Despite the insanity, you will be sobbing. *Love You Forever* reminds you that children get old, and so do their parents—but not before every possible emotional boundary is crossed.

Thanks, book! Let's see ... It's Tuesday night, you had a long day at work, and got home late. You had a total of forty-five minutes with your kid tonight, and the last five of it was a grim warning that everyone you love will die.

You won't sleep tonight, and it won't be because you're masturbating.

 Remember: Nobody dies in *Goodnight Moon*.

SH*TTY MOM: HERE TO HELP

Multinational Corporations That Provide Free Childcare aka How to Write a Book Called *Sh*tty Mom* Without Spending the Entire Advance on Babysitters

Sometimes you have to work instead of parent. Dad is working. Or with his other kids. Or watching football. Or on the lam—tens of thousands of dollars behind in child support. Sitters are expensive, and the grandparents are far away, frail, or dead. You may have a friend, but you can't waste her on this. Your car is making noises or, next month you are moving. She must be saved for something besides a few hours of computer work.

What you need is a contained space that your kids cannot exit without your knowledge. A space with a play area, food, reasonable lighting, and a place to put your laptop. Also, it needs to be free.

The park is no good. You can't see the screen in the sun's glare. And the park is open space—you'll put your headphones on, zone out for twenty minutes, and then look up to find that your kid has wandered off. You don't want to read message board comments about the news reports of a child disappearing while his mother was on Facebook. (That's what everyone will assume, even if your weren't. But you probably were.)

What's a Sh*tty Mom to do? Aside from your local gym/play dumps, try one of these:

McDonald's

McDonald's gets it. For no extra charge, they provide a jungle gym, toys made in China, Wi-Fi, and your own writing desk. And no time limit. Even better, the PlayPlace is too cramped for parents to join their kids on the slides. McDonald's understands that if you actually wanted to play with your kids, you'd be at the park.

McDonald's even offers healthy kids' meals, with apple slices. They are for show, so you can tell yourself that you tried. Because kids are all about Happy Meals, and Happy Meals are all about french fries. And that's fine. The unspoken agreement you've made with your children is that Mom gets to wear headphones and they get to eat fries. This teaches kids another life lesson: When authority figures aren't paying attention, they can do bad things. It's the first step to a well-compensated life of unprosecuted white-collar crime.

IKEA

IKEA should let you leave your kid in a children's model bedroom, while you work at a desk in one of their model home offices. What better way to show off the functionality of both rooms?

Oh well. The next best thing is Småland, IKEA's drop-off play area for short children. (They have a strict height limit that will exclude a tall seven-year-old.)

Unfortunately, Småland has a time limit, and IKEA makes you carry a tracking device so that they can summon you in an emergency or if you're five seconds late. Even worse, there's often a waiting list, which means you'll have time to shop with your kid at IKEA. In that event, a babysitter might be cheaper.

On the plus side, their play structures have never been found to contain trace amounts of MRSA. (Sorry to bring that up, but jeez, McDonald's.) Once you check in your child, go to the café. The coffee is cheap and the meatballs are Swedish.

But work fast, they are tracking you.

(Note: Single moms, you can't afford to hire a sitter every time a horny, divorced dad wants to crawl in your pants. Meet him at IKEA for coffee and meatballs. If there's no chemistry, having to get your kid out of Småland is a perfect excuse to end the date.)

Chuck E. Cheese's

This is a reverse recommendation, because Chuck E. Cheese's is a terrible place to try to work, and that fact needs to be in print. (Besides, anything written in the presence of a six-foot rat is probably not your best effort.) With the loud machines, noises, and tokens, Chuck E. Cheese's is like Vegas for five-year-olds. It's contained, yes, but it also attracts teenagers. Teens who are loud, bored, and unable to think of any place else to go but Chuck E. Cheese's. They're so young, and yet they have already given up on life. Their despair is distracting.

Furthermore, every procedural show with a story line about a pedophile takes place at an establishment that resembles Chuck E. Cheese's. What do TV crime dramas know that they're not telling us?

 Remember: If we weren't being Sh*tty Moms while writing the book *Sh*tty Mom*, what kind of hypocrites would we be?

CHAPTER 48

When Seeing an Infant Triggers a Mental Illness That Makes You Want to Have Another Baby

You're done. Your youngest is two or three or five . . . it doesn't matter. The point is, you aren't having another one. In fact, this weekend you're going to give away the baby clothes.

Feels good.

Wait. What's that in the stroller? Oh God. It's a newborn. Time stops. Chubby legs, and slow-moving, sticky fingers. Knitted booties, a toothless yawn. And your own child over there . . . he is a giant. He wears sneakers that light up and an Ed Hardy shirt. Your kid talks loud and he talks back. The training wheels are about to come off his bike.

You want to trade him for the baby.

Oh no.

We've established that babies are suicidal, dumb, incontinent, costly, and noisy. No one would invite such a creature into their life unless their brain was sick.

You are suffering from "painnesia," a special kind of amnesia that makes you forget pain. Painnesia causes you to take back an ex, eat at the Olive Garden, or start a blog. (Since when did you enjoy writing?) You are like the surfer who loses a limb to a shark and pledges from the hospital bed to return to the waves, better than ever.

You must talk yourself out of this.

DO SOME MATH.

It's estimated that raising a child to age eighteen costs about

$200,000. Think of what you could do with that much money. Your family could fly first class, forever. You could buy a studio apartment in New York City (well, the Bronx) or a house anywhere in Nevada. Single moms? You could have sex with a thousand-dollar-per-night gigolo—two hundred times. You can't imagine the things a thousand-dollar-per-night gigolo would do to your body.

Did it work? Have you booked a first-class ticket on Singapore Airlines? Did you go to Zillow.com and price homes in North Las Vegas? Did you Netflix *American Gigolo*?

No?

All that, and you'd still rather have a baby? Uh-oh. You are in danger. You need to protect yourself. You can't get pregnant when you have baby hunger. That's like telling someone that you love them—for the first time—during sex. You can't take it back, and one day you will desperately want to.

Right now, you are ironically as vulnerable as an infant. But instead of covering the electrical outlets, you need to cover your outlet.

DON'T HAVE SEX.

Your womb cannot be trusted—it wants a baby. Every month that you don't let your womb have a baby, it cries red tears. (At least according to our Irish grandmother.) The moment your womb realizes your head is in the same space, it will send out a search party to look for sperm. Any sperm. If there is no husband or boyfriend available, your womb will get creative. It will check into seedy hotels that don't wash sheets, it will visit crime scenes with a black light and scrape the walls. Your womb wants to make a nuke and, like Iran, it's casting a wide net in the hunt for ingredients.

You probably shouldn't even sit on a public toilet until this feeling passes.

Remember: When your emotional vitals have stabilized, get a puppy.

Three Lies You Tell Yourself to Justify Having Another Baby

* **"I have so much love to give."** No, you don't. Look at how you snapped at the barista who accidentally put whole milk in your skim latte. Honey, you are tapped out.

* **"My son keeps begging for a sister."** No, your kid is begging for a playmate. Once your child realizes that the loud animal in the Miracle Blanket is his sister, he will be appalled and bitter. You don't want a bitter six-year-old. Bitterness, like alcohol, is for grown-ups.

* **"My other child is growing up so fast, I miss the baby phase!"** Now you sound like one of those dads who manages to get his entire family out of their burning house, then dies because he decided to go back in for the cat. Don't be greedy. You escaped infanthood alive. If your kids are out of diapers, you are practically home free. Enjoy it. You can always get another cat.

CHAPTER 49

Rediscover Your Passion for Violent TV, Movies, and Jokes

You're at a comedy club, having a good time. You haven't gone out much since the baby and it's nice to be around adults. Then the comedian tells a dead baby joke. Instead of laughing, like your old self would have done, you take it seriously. Your stomach tightens and you visualize your baby being put inside that joke's microwave oven. My God, how can people laugh at a time like this? You look around. No one else is joining you in this grim fantasy. They're laughing, they're groaning, they're groan-laughing. In fact, the only thing they're not doing is texting the babysitter, to make sure the baby is not being microwaved.

Put your cell phone down. You are pathetic.

What happened to you? Back in the day, you loved yourself a dead baby joke. In fact, you loved jokes about dead people of all ages! And movies, TV shows, and hip-hop. You knew all the words to Eminem's "Stan"—yes you did. You sang along as Stan tied up his girlfriend, threw her in the back of a truck, and drove her off a pier. "Stan" was your jam!

And look at you now. Cowering in the corner, watching *Law & Order: SVU* through a blanket. Shame on you.

There is a way back. You have to desensitize yourself again. Build calluses on your bleeding heart. The *Sh*tty Mom* Media Guide will have you enjoying the fictional death of innocents in no time.

1. Over-the-top ridiculous
Start with violence that is so ridiculous that even you

can laugh at it. The *Saw* movies are just what the doctor ordered. The protagonist is a lunatic who exacts revenge on douchebags by killing them with comical savagery. The *Saw* maniac chooses his victims precisely because they are assholes. They all deserve to die. In this oeuvre (there are at least six), your heartstrings are safe.

2. Watch YouTube

Let's step away from fiction and turn to YouTube. Specifically, videos on YouTube that feature people hurting themselves in the pursuit of something stupid. You will feel no empathy for the dumbass who miscalculates how far he needs to jump off his roof in order to land in a pool. Unless your kid is a dumbass. Then you must:

2a. Stay Away from YouTube

If you suspect your child may one day attach jumper cables to his balls just to see if he can charge them with the car battery, stay away from YouTube. For you, a click on this site is a terrifying glimpse into the future, which is filled with hospital visits, broken bones, and second-degree burns.

Protect yourself. Like carriers of the Huntington's gene who refuse to get tested because knowing the truth would be too awful, the mother of a dumbass must stay off YouTube.

Proceed to step 3.

3. The Old Testament

It's time to move on to nameless people being killed by their jealous God. Open up the Old Testament and head over to Genesis. Start with the Flood. God kills every person except Noah's family. Then go to Exodus, where God kicks off the first Passover by killing every first-born

Egyptian male. If you're really feeling cocky, go back to Genesis where God nearly talks Abraham into killing his son, Isaac. This story will be especially challenging for moms who underwent multiple IVF treatments, as Isaac was conceived when his mother, Sarah, was ninety years old. How many cycles is that, if you start at age forty?

Once you polish off the Old Testament, you are ready for your final challenge.

4. *Dexter*

Dexter is a show about a wry serial killer who kills other serial killers. The violence is often *Saw*-esque in its ridiculousness, and Dexter is very likeable, plus he has a backstory that will break your mom-heart. However, the other serial killers are reprehensible. They kill women, children, and nice people. Season 4 (with the Trinity Killer) is the equivalent of your finals, your LSATs, and your MCATs combined. *Dexter*'s season 4 will make you long for the carefree days of Cain killing Abel. But if you can watch the whole thing... you are officially back.

Now you can go to a comedy club again.

IF YOU STILL WINCE AT VIOLENCE...

Just wait until you are elderly. You'll be all over these shows when you're a senior, because old people love to see young people get killed. They love their *NCIS*, their *Law & Order*s, and their *CSI*s. The brighter the victim's future, the more satisfying his murder. Why? Because old people are jealous cranks (not unlike God in the Old Testament).

When they're not watching *Law & Order*, they're watching *Judge Judy*. They love it when Judge Judy yells at people. It's their Super Bowl. They make dip, and cheer and holler when Her Honor scores a touchdown. Because that's the only thing old people want to do: yell at young people, then have them convicted of stealing their newspaper. As if young people even read newspapers.

One day you will be the old woman cheering on Dexter and highlighting the slavery parts of the Bible.

 Remember: A life spent wincing at dead baby jokes is not a life worth living.

Warning: Do Not Watch *Intervention*

Or any reality show with addicts—they will set you back years. The addict will often describe a "final straw" that turned her into a junkie. Without fail, the addict will describe an event or condition that exists in your life. You will be unable to sleep at night, convinced your actions are setting your child up for a lifetime of rotting teeth and forced rehab:

Heroin addict: "Things got bad when Mom and Dad got a divorce, and then Mom started bringing home a lot of guys."

You: "Oh great. I'm divorced, and a widower on Match just winked at me."

....

Meth user: "I grew up in a small town with nothing to do."

You: "Oh great. I moved here precisely because I thought a small town would be a great place to raise kids."

....

Crackhead: "Our neighbor molested me."
You: "Oh great. I have neighbors, on both sides, and across the street."

....

Alcoholic: "My mom drank a lot."
You: "Well, at least I'm not an alcoholic. Everyone begins their morning with a gin latte. Right?"

CHAPTER 50

How to Stay Sane During a Horrible News Cycle

It happens a lot. You go online to a news site. A *Huffington Post*, a *Drudge*, a *USA Today*. You want a light dusting of information—maybe a headline plus the first paragraph. Stuff that a functioning adult needs to know: politics... celebrities... maybe a video of a moose in a swimming pool. Instead, your eyes find a horrible story involving a child. A child about the same age as yours. You should close the browser window or shut down the laptop completely—anything but read that story.

You don't.

Instead, you lower yourself feetfirst into another mom's horror and practically become her. You imagine how you would act, wonder if you could keep from killing yourself. You start crying. You hug your kids, who think you are weird or drunk.

The horrible thing about parenting is that you are always one dumb mistake away from unfathomable grief. Forget to check the battery in the smoke detector, trust the wrong coach, or drive into an intersection at the same time as a drunk, and your kid is damaged or gone. Everybody warns new parents about the lack of sleep and the endless expenses but really the worst part is that, for the rest of your life, your heart can be broken.

If you replay each well-publicized crime or accident as if it had happened to your family, you will go mad. And you can't go mad. You have kids to raise, and *Real Housewives* to watch.

AVOID THAT KIND OF NEWS.
In particular, HLN's Nancy Grace must be shunned. There are

some news stories you don't need to be versed on, and she covers all of them.

If you read a child crime story online, do not scroll down to the comments. What's left of your stomach will be sickened by the ferocious hatred aimed at the mother. Men and women alike pile on mom. If the perpetrator is the child's father, it's mom's fault for marrying him. If Anne Frank had lived to read Internet comments, she would have realized that, deep down, people are really assholes.

BE THANKFUL YOU LIVE IN THE TWENTY-FIRST CENTURY.

On the bright side, it's a good time to be a human being! The world is kinder now than any time in history. Unlike your fore-mothers, you will never see your kid sacrificed by Aztecs, tossed into the sea by Spartans, raped by Gauls, speared by Cromwell's men, wedged onto a slave ship headed for the New World, or paralyzed from polio.

So you got that going for you.

YOU AND YOURS WILL PROBABLY DIE OF OLD AGE.

It is likely that a terrible thing will never happen to you and your family. (Unless you are a Kennedy. Then all bets are off.) But for the rest of us, the worrying and what-iffing is for naught. Your kids will be fine. You will be plagued with the usual aging-woman crap: gray pubic hair, veiny Madonna hands, and a hearing loss so annoying that people will stop talking to you.

You ought to "what-if" all the shitty things that are bound to occur, like "What if my kid drops out of college?" or "What if he stays in college and majors in architecture?"

Here's what's probably going to happen: Your child will move back home until he's thirty, marry someone you don't like, name his daughter after the other grandmother, bury you in that cemetery you never cared for, grow old, go bald, and also die. And so on and so forth until mankind itself is undone by global warming or great white sharks.

In other words, you've got lots to look forward to.

 Remember: You are on track to lead a boring life that will never make _Headline News_, and that's good.

CHAPTER 51

Play Trains or Dolls with Your Kids Without Sticking Your Head in the Oven

Pastors often say, "Hate the sin and love the sinner." Similarly, you can love your daughter and hate playing Barbies with her.

Look. You're an adult. You've had sex. You've been to Vegas enough times to legitimately call it "Vegas." Once, you stayed awake for thirty-one hours straight, and twice you've watched porn on your laptop while your mother was in the next room. If you haven't been groped yet by a stranger on a train, you will be.

You've paid your dues.

A woman such as yourself has earned the right to not wield a lightsaber and answer to "Leia." And yet your kids will pester and beg. Be easy on them, they don't get out much. At the moment, you are the coolest person they know, and they like being seen with you.

* **You can do a bad job.** This is trains, not your career. And your kid is not evaluating you for a raise. It's plenty good enough to run the train back and forth on one long track instead of reaching over and running the train on curvy tracks and through bridges and roundabouts. The rule is if you started the activity sitting with your legs crossed, you should finish it sitting with your legs crossed.

* **You can quit after a few minutes.** Sometimes they only need a jump-start. If you put in ten intense and involved

minutes, you may be able to scoot away unnoticed and they will play on their own for a half hour.

* **Background audio.** This is a great time to introduce your kid to music from your youth: Springsteen, Prince, Madonna, U2, Nirvana, David Bowie, Foo Fighters. (If the Foo Fighters represent music from your youth, the Springsteen Moms request that you stop reading for a moment and flip yourself off. Thank you.)

* **Um, isn't this Dad shit?** "Wait till Dad gets home" used to be about beatings. For this generation, it's about play-time. Most women do more than 50 percent of the par-enting and housework. Shooting bad guys is Dad shit.

* **The desire to play with you won't last long.** If your kid is two or older, he is never more than ten years away from denying you in public and ignoring you at home. One of these playtimes really will be your last.

 Remember: You don't have to be great at this because Dad is supposed to be the fun one.

Always Deny: Your Kid Cheats at Improv

Having conversations with your preschooler is like being stuck in an improv scene with the worst partner on earth. Let's say your child approaches you in the kitchen while you are making breakfast.

"Mom, oh no! Our plane is on fire!"

Your four-year-old daughter has just sprung an improv scene on you. Hope you're ready. She has given you a location (a plane), and a circumstance (flames). From the way she is crouching, the two of you are passengers together on this doomed Hindenburg. The first rule in improv is "Never deny."

"Oh my gosh," you say, looking around, "our plane is on fire!" OK, you aren't exactly Robin Williams, but you are playing along. Good for you.

"And the plane has lots of feet and the feet are very hot," she says.

Aha, more information from your partner! Not only are you flying in a plane that is on fire, but the plane, for reasons that may never be revealed, has feet. Lots of them. And those feet are hot (probably due to the fire).

"Well, we should put shoes on the plane," you say, advancing the scene.

"Mom," your daughter sighs, "planes don't wear shoes."

Duh. You moron.

CHAPTER 52

The Very Last Thing You Should Do Before You Give Birth

You're thirty-nine weeks along—this part is almost over. The missed period, the "yes" on the stick, the sonogram, the folic acid, the omega-3 oils, the nuchal and results, the peeing, the amnio and results, the stretch-marks lotion, the secret Sunday sips of merlot, the men giving up their seats, the sleeping on your back, the nursery, the best stroller, the mother-in-law's favorite boy name being Francis, the baby shower, the cloth diapers you will use once then toss.

You are almost ready. There's only one thing left to do: have your roots done.

The first few hours after the baby comes, you will be in a blurry, ecstatic state. Flush with new mama-love and painkillers. Then the anesthesia or epidural will wear off. You'll need to pee. The bathroom will be four feet away and to get there you'll need a walker. During this trek, you will understand your vagina is being held together by stitches. If you had a C-section, there is a thin-lipped smile across your stomach. You look like what you are: a childbirth survivor.

Now the outlines of your new life are growing clear and crisp. Body halves held together by threads, the vague memory of that shit taken in the delivery room (and in front of your husband). Breasts that are full and leaking a milk stain down your shirt, in the shape of Chile.

What you need right now is to look in the mirror and think, "God damn. At least my hair looks good."

Make an appointment, and do it quick in case the baby comes

early. If you can afford more procedures, get a pedicure and wax your legs. Basically, make it so that for the first six weeks, you don't need to check on any hair below your waist. If you bend over for a calf shave too soon, you might get a glimpse of the vaginal damage before the swelling subsides, and your despair will be unending.

For this reason, bikini or Brazilian wax is not advised. You need coverage.

 Remember: To steal an aphorism from Alcoholics Anonymous: "First things first." Roots, then baby.

ABOUT THE AUTHORS

Each of the four authors is, in her own way, a Sh*tty Mom.

LAURIE KILMARTIN is an Emmy-nominated writer for *CONAN* on TBS, and a stand-up comedian who's appeared on *CONAN*, *Last Comic Standing*, *Jimmy Kimmel Live*, and *Comedy Central*. She lives in Los Angeles with her son.

KAREN MOLINE is a journalist and author who has written over two dozen nonfiction books as well as two novels, *Lunch* and *Belladonna*. Karen and her son live in New York City.

ALICIA YBARBO is a four-time Emmy Award–winning producer. She's worked for NBC Sports, ABC's *The View*, and NBC's *Today* show, where she's been since 2000. She lives in New York City with her husband and their two children.

MARY ANN ZOELLNER is a three-time Emmy Award–winning producer who has worked at NBC News for sixteen years. Prior to that she worked for the *Jenny Jones Show* and *Larry King Live*. Mary Ann lives in New York City with her husband and their two daughters.